SEVENTY-FIVE FEELING ALIVE

Travelling Solo As A Septuagenarian

JL COLEY

Some men see things as they are and say why, I dream things that never were and say why not?

George Bernard Shaw

CONTENTS

In The Beginning
South America
    Peru
    Bolivia
    Chile
    Argentina
    Uruguay
    Brazil
Central America
    Costa Rica
    Panama
    Guatemala
    Belize
    Mexico
An Aside: I'm Not a Cocktail Girl
United States of America
    Southern Sights and Sounds
Acknowledgements

In The Beginning

I remember learning about South America in geography lessons and saying to myself, one day I want to visit. I've always had wanderlust, possibly inherited from my mum whose favourite book as a child was Swiss Family Robinson which she kept hidden under the desk in school, frequently getting into trouble for secretly reading it instead of paying attention. Mrs Hudson, my secondary school teacher, didn't exactly fill me with a desire to see the world; I can picture her now, a shock of white hair, long skirt, navy cotton twill jacket, always with a silver brooch in the shape of Africa on the lapel, striding along like an intrepid traveller. My learning about Africa, obviously her passion, in the first year, passed me by but then, in the second year, we began to study South America. There was something about the continent which captured my imagination, I could picture the events I was learning about; the conquistadors from Spain and Portugal who travelled to the Americas to conquer foreign lands, the discovery of the ancient Incan empire in Peru, the attempts to sail round the treacherous Cape Horn and open up new trade routes. In my mind I was there, living it.

What better way to celebrate becoming a septuagenarian than to set off on a type of adventure I'd never undertaken before, a solo trip for an extended period. It was never meant to be one of those 'I need to find myself' sort of trips, a spiritual experience to find my karma, but there was something about being in my seventies which made me want to confront my age, to prove to myself there was still life in the old dog yet, at the same time challenging how an older person might be perceived, and South America seemed the obvious choice.

I'd reached the age when finding travel companions had become more difficult; bereavement, ill health, finances, family commitments, being factors for others. I also found that, whilst you might still enjoy a wide circle of friends, choosing a companion you'd be happy to spend a prolonged time with as one gets older, is not altogether straightforward, particularly as I'd decided six weeks would be a good length holiday. Anyway, I rather fancied going by myself, there was more of a sense of adventure about undertaking a long solo trip. Capturing the excitement I'd felt in geography lessons would be even more meaningful if I were travelling solo.

I gave myself a good talking to about double and triple checking everything, from a thorough look in the safe before I moved to the next hotel, to making sure the zips on my bum bag with passport, credit card and currency in, were always securely in place. There wouldn't be a companion with me to ask if I'd forgotten anything, consequently, it was entirely up to me. Also, I made myself accept that things might not always go smoothly; lost luggage, missed connections, theft, delayed flights. My mantra would be 'Go with the flow.'

People commented on how brave they thought I was, however, I was reassured by the encouragement from my children whose attitude was very much, 'Good for you, go for it Mum!' Had they been worried, it might have been more concerning for me, (but I would have done it anyway).

And so, after months of planning, I set off on my solo adventure.

SOUTH AMERICA

Peru

Of all the six countries on my itinerary this is in my top two; visions of brightly coloured ponchos and smiley, weathered faces occupy my imagination of the ancient Inca kingdom and the wealth it held thanks to the rich source of gold.

I arrive at my Lima hotel, ready for a good night's sleep to set me up for my six weeks adventure. I'd decided not to sleep on the plane, thinking I would then be ready for a long, deep sleep; however, it isn't to be. A combination of excitement and different time zones are against me and, despite putting the light out and closing my eyes in an attempt to get some shuteye at nine o'clock, sleep eludes me.

When my alarm goes off at seven the next morning, I look back on a restless night with maybe four hours sleep. Not a great start to my trip. Perhaps it's a lesson to be learnt for subsequent trips, grab some shut eye when you can regardless of time zones. I know of some travellers who can be disciplined about sticking to sleep patterns, making sure they alter their watches to the upcoming time zones as soon as they've stepped on the plane, but not me. Grab the zzzs whenever I feel like it, is my mantra from now on.

The first day is taking me on a guided tour of Peru's capital city; we visit the main square with LIMA in large letters, the cathedral and the very first post box in Peru, the mouth of a polished brass lion's head set in a wall. My guide draws my attention to the many decorative balconies as we stroll around, a legacy of the Moorish culture. They were an integral feature of each house, designed to allow the women of the family to view what was happening outside in the street below but without them being seen in public. They also give Lima the name, City of Balconies. I'm also introduced to a flower I've never come across before, called Yesterday, Today, Tomorrow because of the three distinct colours of its flowers, purple, lilac and white, already in bloom despite the time of year being early Spring.

We visit the Museo Larco, a museum housing artefacts from Peru's early history. Inside there are over five thousand stone portrait vessels on display, each one with distinctive features, although all in terracotta, cream, and black. The visit to the museum is a great starting point and I begin to immerse myself in the ancient history of the country, despite my tiredness. The artefacts, along with an ample collection of silver and gold jewellery, give me an insight into the Andean culture, and I realise, by the end of the day, my guide has fitted in a remarkable amount during the short visit to Lima. However, there is no time to draw breath before I'm driven to the airport to move on to the next leg of the trip.

One thing I was a little nervous about when planning my trip, was getting myself from A to B with only a smattering of Spanish to rely on. I needn't have worried, my driver and guide give me clear instructions where to go after I check in; up the escalator, turn right to passport control then follow signs to Security. Having negotiated the way there, I unclip the bum bag containing all my valuables and take off shoes with my orthotics, in order to avoid making the machine bleep. (I resolve on my next trip, should I get through this one without a hitch, to pack them in future and wear a pair of slip ons for flights.) The laptop is removed from the backpack, sending sheets of paper with my itinerary on flying. Flustered, I quickly scoop everything up and place them in the tray. I've been through this procedure countless times but being by myself and wanting to get it right, for some reason makes me nervous.

Having safely negotiated getting airside and reaching the departure lounge, I begin to relax. The first hurdle has been overcome and I'm still in one piece.

The next morning, I awake in the Sacred Valley; the flight had been quick and easy the night before and I'd been met by a delightful young woman from the tour company and a driver to take me to my hotel.

I've been forewarned about the potential problem of altitude and am guessing that's why the travel agent has arranged a two night stay here before my visit to Machu Picchu, to give my body a chance to acclimatise. However, I can feel the effects of it already, a slight tightness in the chest and a little breathless. There is a supply of mate tea in the lobby for guests, to help combat the problem, and I take full advantage of it. As my sleep pattern has still to adapt to the difference in time zones, I'm happy to stay in this beautiful area and, as a precursor, learn a little about Peru and its culture.

Our first stop of the day is Chinchero, to the market there, to watch a demonstration of prepping dyes for weaving. In the words of Michael Caine, not many people may know this, but blue is made by using the excrement and urine from the children. Evidently adults' consumption of beer makes wee the wrong colour to use, so the wee (pardon the pun) ones have to provide the wherewithal. I also learn the difference between an alpaca and a llama; the former has smaller stubby faces and short ears while the latter's face is longer, and the ears are also bigger. Did Michael Caine know this gem of wisdom I wonder?

On the way to our next stop, I notice white patches on the hillside in the distance, salt flats. I don't know at the time, but they'll be nothing compared to what I'll see when I move on to Bolivia. We pass roadside stalls displaying colourful hats and scarves arranged on hat stands, being gently blown by the breeze, I can see mountains in the background with snowy tops, the sky is a brilliant blue with just a few patchy clouds punctuating it; I can't quite believe I'm here.

We make a short stop at Moray to look deep down into a large area carved out in concentric circles into the land beneath us. These are pre-Incan and were agricultural terraces, believed to be an experimental farm system from five hundred years ago and providing a microclimate for growing crops. I turn down the offer of walking down the path to take a closer look; the slight tightness is still there in my chest, and I don't want to take any chances.

My attention is diverted by my guide to what looks like a large shed in the distance, on the other side of the hill. I assume it's a barn, probably housing grain and farm machinery. 'That is Mil,' she points out, 'one of the most prestigious restaurants in the world.' I can't help but show my surprise, there appears to be nothing else nearby except open land. 'People come from miles around just to eat there,' she tells me. 'Peru is very famous for its culinary excellence.'

Our next stop, Ollantaytambo, was built by the Incas as a stronghold, one which even the Spanish couldn't penetrate when they arrived in the fifteenth century. My guide is insistent we should climb the fifty-seven flights of steps to the top and reassures me I can take as much time as I like. Having opted out of the walk down to the terraces at Moray, I think to myself, daft to come all this way and not take advantage of another thing on offer, so I hesitantly agree.

She is very understanding about my constant need to stop and get my breath back as we ascend the steep, winding route with large, rough-hewn stones creating the path. The altitude at three thousand eight hundred metres isn't easy for me, she on the other hand scales the climb like a mountain goat. We stop at one point, and she introduces me to the value of cocoa leaves to help with the altitude problem. She offers some and advises me not to chew them unless I want my teeth go brown but instead to store a few in the pouch between the end of my bottom teeth and my cheek. I readily accept the leaves from her. I'd researched how I could get medication for helping with altitude before I started the trip, but ones like Diamox aren't available over the counter or on prescription, only on the internet, and I hadn't wanted to risk buying tablets online.

Having reached the top, we stop for a well-earned rest and to admire the view; as I look back down to where we've come from, I get a sense of how difficult it would have been for marauding invaders to penetrate this bastion.

If going up was demanding then coming down is even more so, with the deep uneven steps and a flimsy rope rail to hold onto. But when we eventually get to the bottom, my knees have survived, and I'm pleased I'd been persuaded to do the climb.

Needless to say, on returning to the hotel, I make use of the hammock in the grounds; I lie back to admire the beautiful gardens around me, while gently swaying from side to side, at the same time giving my feet a well-earned rest.

We'd stopped for a buffet lunch during the day, consequently I skip dinner and head for the steam room instead. I feel a cold starting, not what I would welcome at the start of my adventure. Before long, the heat makes me sleepy, and I go to bed early; my body has worked hard today, and I feel like I'm ready to drop off. I have to because tomorrow I'm moving on again, to the mighty Machu Picchu, the well documented and famous settlement of the Incas.

I wake early feeling refreshed and look out of my window at a cloudless pink and pale blue sky. My brief time in the Sacred Valley has been the perfect start to my trip and has given my body the opportunity to acclimatise, as well as introducing me to the Incan civilisation.

I make my way to the restaurant, enjoying strolling through the hotel gardens, taking in the sight of unfamiliar trees and shrubs. I do like breakfasts in hotels and make sure I always fuel up for the day. Today, my choice is a refreshing pineapple tea with kumquat, a plate of fruit, cheese omelette, pancake with maple syrup, and obligatory mate tea. Now I won't have to worry about lunch!

The guide takes me to Ollantaytambo station and sees me to my seat on the train. After making sure the porter has stowed my suitcase safely away, she bids me goodbye, having already explained I'll be met off the train by a new guide and my luggage taken care of by the next hotel. I've only been in Peru for three days but here I am, moving on to my third location.

As the train begins to climb we pass rivers coursing through the hillside, then there is a brief stop at a railway station to allow a small group of passengers to disembark; not for them the comfort of a train compartment, but walkers ready to start their journey along the Inca trail, a route following the path taken by the Incans many centuries before, and now a rite of passage for many a backpacker.

Machu Picchu is busy by the time I arrive, but the site is so vast it isn't long before my guide finds a relatively quiet area, and I can enjoy it without being in the company of hordes of people. I'm glad I'm wearing my hiking trainers; the terrain is rocky and uneven in places, although in others the walking is along flat grassy pathways and easy to manoeuvre.

While my guide talks about the importance historically of the settlement, I allow my gaze to go for a wander, trying to take in all I can. I see a group on the side of the hill, its members are arriving through the Sun Gate in their matching bright green T shirts, having just finished the Inca trail. As they get nearer, I can see how exhausted they are but at the same time they look triumphant, having completed the route.

Built as a retreat for Inca rulers, Machu Picchu housed a community which thrived for a hundred years or so until the Spanish Conquest. The ruins still give a sense of what it was like living there during that time; steeped terraces divided by stone walls, the remains of buildings, some with walls made out of roughly hewn rocks, while others, like the high priest's house, built with shaped, smoother stones. I let my mind run freely, picturing what the scene might have been like at that time. I imagine people going about their daily routines and can almost hear their voices when I close my eyes; the high priest in daily prayer, the servant at his master's beck and call, busying himself with all the chores he has to complete, llamas being herded, and the familiar sounds of children playing.

I'm staying in a rather pukka all-inclusive hotel, an extravagance I'd decided to treat myself to. There is a pisco tasting before dinner and about to begin so I hurriedly wash and change then head to the bar. We're each given a measure of pisco to try neat to start with, although the clear white spirit is mostly known as being the basis of a pisco sour. The taste is like a superior quality brandy; it is surprisingly smooth and very drinkable. Next our bartender explains how it can be served with different mixes to complement the taste, rather like other spirits. We try the most well-known version with lemon juice, egg white and sugar syrup, shaken over ice in a cocktail shaker. A good start to the evening.

My dinner menu sounds delicious; I go for a starter of grilled trout fillet with a chia seed crust, and yellow chilli pepper sauce with apple, then fish again for the main course; grilled white paiche from the Peruvian jungle with chestnut and cashew Cajun puree. And to finish off, rice tamale, pumpkin souffle with carob ice cream. I can understand why Peruvian cooking is so highly rated if this is an example. My choice of accompanying wine is from Chile, and I see there's also a dessert wine from Undurraga, a vineyard I'm supposed to be visiting at some point on my itinerary. I decide, as the hotel is all inclusive, to push the boat out and have a glass of that as well to go with my souffle.

Later I return to my room from dinner to find a large scented candle in a decorative bowl has been lit in my room to keep the mosquitoes at bay; a nicer touch than the plug-in insect repellents installed in some hotels.

As my train the following day isn't until late afternoon, I use the morning to stroll round the Machu Picchu site again. There are pretty flowers and shrubs to admire, llamas ambling freely, and mountains all around, including the tall Huayna Picchu. My visit also includes a pass to climb it, from where I'm assured there are spectacular views, but at an altitude of over two thousand metres, although not as high as Ollantaytambo, I decide to opt out and view it instead from my perch on a grassy bank. Although the mountains surrounding me are dark and imposing, I feel a sense of peace here and I can understand people's views about Machu Picchu holding a certain mystic allure.

There is just enough time to browse the tourist market in Aguas Calientes before my train back to Cusco departs. I'm tempted by a number of souvenirs on sale but restrict myself to buying a woolly hat in bright yellow, jade and maroon, to coordinate with my puffer jacket. It is very Peruvian in its colourfulness and will act as a great memory of this special place.

My guided tour of Cusco, once the capital of Peru before Lima, the next morning starts at the Santo Domingo convent, a good example of how both Incan and Spanish influences are still present in this city. The convent's walls are surrounded by the remains of an Incan temple, similarly a church we visit is built on the ruins of another. The Vatican decreed that all Inca buildings should be destroyed during the Spanish Conquest, however the edict wasn't always implemented, consequently a number of reminders of the Incan civilisation exist to this day. There are the remains of the Saqsaywaman fortress built high above the city; its gigantic stones needed one thousand men per stone to transport them, making the stones at Stone Henge look minute in comparison. The legacy of the Incas and the Spanish Conquest can also be seen in one street name called Calle (Spanish for street) Intikijllu (from the Incan language).

On our way back to the car, the path is lined with distinctive looking trees, which are unfamiliar to me; their bark is a deep red and they have grey green leaves, whilst their branches are spread wide, the ones near the bottom lying low to the ground, not unlike a mesquite tree. My guide tells me they are Andean Paper trees, named because of their thin paper like bark. Spotting new things like trees I've never come across before, is all part of this wonderful experience.

My last afternoon in Cusco is free; I'd hoped to visit San Pedro market but am told it's closed at the moment. Instead, I wander down to the shop in my hotel and peruse the scarves. There's a sale on and I'm tempted to do my Xmas shopping now. Yes, I really do mean Xmas! I like giving gifts from places on my travels; in New Zealand it was possum socks and manuka honey for my nearest and dearest.

Alpaca scarves from a reputable shop, (I'd been forewarned about the quality in the markets), seem like a desirable choice and the colours and range are gorgeous. The only problem is how to transport them with me on the remainder of my trip, I still have nearly five weeks of touring to go. I bite the bullet and decide to send them back to the UK by post, seven of them in all. Doesn't sound like much and certainly isn't weight wise but the bulk would make them impossible for me to fit into my case. My plan seems like a clever idea but as it turns out, the postage costs almost as much as the scarves. Definitely a lesson learnt.

It's late afternoon by now and I realise I haven't had anything to eat since breakfast. I often forego lunch as such, taking a muffin and piece of fruit from the restaurant in the morning, but today I've been totally absorbed in getting the scarves sorted, consequently I've forgotten to eat. I recall seeing a Por Kilo eatery just off the main square, the Plaza de Armas, and head that way. I first came across this type of restaurant in Rio de Janeiro; there is no menu, instead the meal is a buffet, and as the name suggests, you pay for however much your plate of food weighs, similar in that sense to the idea of Pick and Mix sweets. I've enjoyed the Peruvian cuisine, and it seems a good way to end my stay in Cusco. Disappointingly, I discover the restaurant doesn't open until later; instead, my hunger has to be satisfied with quesadillas elsewhere.

The train taking me on to the next location of my itinerary is a throwback to travelling in style in a bygone era. Each 'guest' is accompanied to her/his seat; on being shown mine I'm greeted by a comfy looking upholstered seat with a table in front of it, covered by the most brilliant white tablecloth I've ever seen. On it a place setting has been laid ready for my lunch. My fellow passengers around me excitedly take their seats and we all introduce ourselves. The long eleven-hour journey to Puno, on the shores of Lake Titicaca, means we'll be sharing each other's company for quite some time.

As soon as we have set off, I stroll along to the observation car, a beautiful open-ended carriage with panoramic glass windows on either side, and furnished in polished wood and brass fittings, which shine resplendently in the bright Peruvian sun. It's a popular choice and before long I'm joined by other travellers, all vying to get the best view, although at this stage all we can see is the suburbs of Cusco. Music is starting in the bar in the next carriage, already choc a bloc with other passengers. I manage to get the last seat and am immediately served a pisco sour. This, the music (for those of you old enough to remember the group, dressed and sounding like Los Paraguayos), and the bowl of nuts I've been given to accompany my drink, get me nicely in the mood.

Our train continues on its way, through the Altiplano, the highest plateau in the world outside of Tibet. Flat grassy plains are surrounded by mountains, and the sky seems to get closer as we climb higher and higher.

We stop to stretch our legs at the highest point on our journey, four thousand, three hundred and thirty metres, and I feel, if I jumped, I'd be able to touch the clouds. The temperature is comfortable, the sky is blue, and I have to pinch myself to believe I really am experiencing this. We climb aboard again and hear the announcement that lunch is about to be served. I take a sneaky peak in the observation car again, by now empty, and take in the glorious uninterrupted view.

I would like to share with you what was on the menu, but I haven't got a clue; my idyll was suddenly turned on its head when, after the first course of my three-course meal, out of nowhere, my breathing becomes shallow and I'm struggling to cope. My main course is put in front of me, and I try to eat but anything restricting my diaphragm only makes breathing more difficult. I can't finish my meal and take a walk along the carriages in the hope that my body will be able to work more efficiently if I'm standing.

Oxygen cylinders are placed at the end of each carriage and, whilst I don't want to make a fuss, I'm aware I need something to help me cope with that feeling of having a heavy weight on my chest. I decide not to return to my seat but instead find a quieter carriage to sit in, one with only a handful of passengers. I explain to a staff member about the difficulty I'm experiencing, and he fetches an oxygen cylinder. 'Only for twenty minutes,' he tells me, before attaching the plastic mask on my face.

It gives me some respite but at the end of my allotted time, the problem is still there. A passenger with an Australian accent approaches me and proceeds to take my pulse then gets me to explain the problem; it turns out he is a surgeon from Sydney. 'Just a moment,' he says and returns to his seat to talk briefly with his travelling companions. 'Have you heard of Diamox?' He asks, on his return. I nod my head. 'We have four spare tablets we can give you, that should help.'

To say I'm grateful for his assistance would be an understatement. 'And another twenty minutes of oxygen shouldn't be a problem,' he adds, and immediately calls the staff member to let me have some more.

Whilst my breathing is still shallow, I'm feeling slightly better by now. I sit quietly for the remainder of the train journey and hope I'll feel okay in time. I'm aware though that Puno is actually at a higher altitude than Cusco.

Much to my relief, there is an oxygen cylinder sitting in the lobby of my hotel when we reach Puno. The very kind Aussie is also staying there; he tells me it's safe to have another twenty minutes, and by the time I get to bed, I'm feeling much better, although the tightness hasn't gone completely. If the truth be known I've been frightened by my experience.

The next day is a full tour to visit two islands, Uros, and Taquile. The former sits on a bed of dried reeds; it's an odd feeling when we first alight from our boat and stand on it. There is a slight bouncy feel, a sensation of never being completely still and I'm glad when we're invited to sit down and given a brief talk on how the Amaira people live there. Traditional methods of cooking over an open fire with clay pots are used, however there are some mod cons. I can see solar panels around and we're told they provide the lighting and power to watch TV.

We take a short ride on a boat also made from reeds. I'm persuaded to have my photo taken rowing the boat, posing in traditional garb of poncho and felt hat, but the expression on my face shows I'm still not feeling too chipper.

We move onto the next island, Taquile, for lunch; quinoa soup and fish from the lake, then have the option of walking round the island. I decide to sit instead and take in the view.

The coastline reminds me of the Amalfi coast; rocky cliffs dropping down into the sea, beautiful trees standing tall on the hillside, and colourful flowers amongst shrubs of different shapes and sizes. I get chatting to an Australian couple, who like me choose to sit rather than take a walk; it turns out they're regular visitors to my area of London to visit relatives who happen to live in the road next to where I used to live. Of all of the gin joints in all of the towns……!

Again, I take advantage of the oxygen in the lobby on my return to the hotel, and having eaten lunch out, I forego dinner and retire early to my room to pack for the next day.

There is a fire in the hearth when I come down to breakfast; the nights are still cold despite the temperate weather during the day. I'm hungry, having missed dinner and not being able to finish my lunch on the train. I fill my plate from the vast array of fruit on offer and have a bowl of cereal as well. I forego the bacon and egg and instead go for crepes made to order, liberally covered with honey this time. All is washed down by a juice and the obligatory mate tea. At last, I'm beginning to feel human again.

I see the green oxygen cylinder in the lobby while I wait for my driver; it has been my life saver, although I still don't feel completely right. Hopefully, I will in time, although I'm aware the altitude is going to be high at my next stay-over. My fleeting time in Peru has been everything I'd hoped for, its history fascinating, the scenery spectacular, and the people warm and welcoming. However, I'm excited to move on, because, after ten days here, I am crossing Lake Titicaca and starting the next leg of my adventure, vamos Bolivia!

Machu Pichu

Stone portrait vessels from the Museo Larco

Sacred Valley

Arros Islands - Lake Titicaca

Bolivia

The minibus is skirting Lake Titicaca, the world's highest navigable lake, then heading for the border, a journey of around one hundred miles. My travel companions are an Aussie couple and a family of three from Israel. I'm enjoying taking in the lakeside views as we drive; the water is clear and as still as a mill pond, and the journey is traffic free.

There's a slight hold up when we reach the border while my Israeli travel companions get the visas they need before they can cross into Bolivia. We're being picked up by another minibus on the other side; while we wait, I look around and can see that everything appears to be more worn, I guess a sign of the difference in wealth between the two countries.

Our first stop is the tourist town of Copacabana. We've been travelling for some time by now and I'm glad of the chance to stretch my legs and take a look round. 'Ah a wedding!' I announce, pointing to the car adorned with flowers in front of the basilica steps.

'No, not a wedding, a new car,' our guide says. I look at her, a puzzled expression on my face. She explains, 'It is a custom to bring your new car here and have it blessed by a priest. That is why it is decorated.' I watch as a priest arrives and proceeds to circle the car, chanting solemnly in hushed tones, while the new owner looks on like a proud father, watching his baby being baptised.

We move along to the fruit market where the guide has told us photos aren't allowed. 'It is people's work area, they do not like tourists taking their photos,' she adds. We move through the stalls overladen with brightly coloured fruit and vegetables, some of which are unfamiliar to me. I forget her words and take a snap of the produce on display, resulting in the workers giving me a frosty look. I mouth, 'Lo siento', then hurriedly catch up with the rest of my group.

The next leg of our journey is by boat on Titicaca to Isla del Sol from where we've been told there will be beautiful views of the lake. I'm tempted to stay on board when we dock at the island, the seventy odd steps we'll have to climb makes me wary, with my breathing still not feeling right. My rather large Aussie co-passenger encourages me. 'Come on, let's give it a go,' he says. We start our ascent and, like my visit to Ollantaytambo, I'm glad I've been persuaded because the views really are spectacular. We stop to receive a blessing from the local shaman, and my Aussie buddy is asked to remove his baseball cap; this is a religious ceremony, he is reminded and has to be treated with the utmost respect.

By the time we return to the boat, I'm hungry and am delighted to see lunch has been laid out ready for us. There are only seven of us on board a boat which can probably carry a hundred passengers. The buffet lunch is plentiful and the food tasty. I go back for second helpings; it's obvious I still haven't satisfied my appetite from the day before.

Later, we disembark and climb back into our minibus for the final leg of our trip. Traffic is horrendous getting through El Alto, the large city adjacent to La Paz where we're heading, and our journey is considerably delayed; it seems like a long time since we left our hotel this morning.

By mid evening, we have eventually arrived. None of my companions is staying at my hotel and I'm glad to be the first one dropped off. I'm also relieved to find my trusty friend, the green cylinder, is there to greet me, but this time in my room. The oxygen is complimentary, but should I require a second cylinder, the cost would be twenty-five dollars. My stay is only for two nights so I'm confident one will be adequate. I have to smile at the progression, or should it be digression, in the availability of oxygen; on the train the guard was hesitant about me having more than a twenty minute dose, at the Puno hotel I had free access, albeit in the lobby, and now here it's on tap in my room, giving me free rein.

I make myself unpack first then lie down and hope the oxygen cylinder is easy to use. It is, and I enjoy twenty minutes before getting ready for bed. There's certainly no need for dinner tonight, not after all I ate at lunch.

La Paz is the highest administrative capital in the world at three and a half thousand metres above sea level, and, as it's my only full day here, the itinerary is going to be a busy one. Our first stop is a drive from the centre of the city to Moon Valley where erosion has worn away a large part of a mountain. It is unusual in that the mountain is made of clay rather than rock, and what's left is a strange looking site. There are raised wooden walkways weaving through the area, giving it the feel of an archaeological dig; I wander around and think how it could easily be a scene from a Stars Wars movie with nothing but craggy outlines of beigy grey rock, rather like giant stalagmites. My guide tells me Moon Valley won't exist in ten years time and will all be washed away because of the constituency of the earth and the amount of rainfall La Paz gets. The city is criss crossed by hundreds of rivers, there is a constant threat of floods and landslides.

We stop off at the home of ceramicist, Mario Sarabia; he uses the clay from the local area to create his pieces. Sarabia talks to us briefly before getting back to his two apprentices who are busily working away. We take a wander through the showroom looking at the items for sale. Shame I'm only in my second country of six, much as it's lovely to look at his beautiful artefacts, the pieces would be far too heavy to carry with me on my tour.

Our next stop is the station, no, not the metro or train, but the cable car. The ariel tramway system is a popular way of getting around the city, its eight lines, with more in the planning stage, are all colour coordinated, making it easy to navigate. Senior citizens get a discount, consequently it is a popular mode of transport for older people. I explain to my guide how lucky we are in London to have free travel after a certain time of day on busses, tube, and trains in the city.

It seems strange to be in a busy metropolis, travelling high above the traffic, to get from A to B, and passing other commuters in cable cars going in the opposite direction. Most of them stare straight ahead, seemingly absorbed in their own thoughts but then I see a small child with a beaming smile waving to me from a cable car travelling in the opposite direction. I wave back and give him a smile in return.

I'd decided to set myself a challenge on this trip, to travel on as many different modes of transport as possible. Consequently, I'm pleased to add another to my list today. So far, the list includes Shank's pony, lift, escalator, travelator, plane, car, train, coach, and boat. Hopefully, I'll be able to add a few more before my holiday's over.

We stop to browse a museum dedicated to precious metals and I have a photo taken there with a woman wearing a bowler hat. The headwear was introduced to Bolivia by a British gentleman and is now recognised as part of the country's traditional folk attire.

We find our way to the Witches Market, a well-known feature of the city, patronised by a large number of stalls selling all sorts of potions for a wealth of ailments. It's beginning to rain heavily and most of the items on sale are being covered up. I ask about something to help me combat altitude sickness, thinking there might be a herbal remedy on sale, but my guide instead takes me to a nearby chemist. My fourth newfound friend, after mate tea, cocoa leaves and oxygen, awaits me and I'm relieved to at last get hold of some Diamox of my own to resolve the altitude problem.

We just make it back to the car before the heavens open even more and a torrent of rain begins to fall. Visibility out of my hotel bedroom window is so poor, because of the amount of rain falling, I can't see the building across the road. Consequently, I'm relieved to learn there's a food court in the same complex as my hotel and I can find somewhere to eat without the need to go outside and endure the deluge. The eating area is crowded with customers wanting to take shelter from the weather outside, however the staff are super efficient, and it isn't long before I get served.

On returning to my room, I go through the now ritual of having my dose of oxygen and then pack my case for my departure the next morning. It's been a quick visit to La Paz but certainly worthwhile.

I sleep the sleep of the gods and wake up feeling refreshed. I'm leaving Bolivia's capital city to catch a flight; there's another experience awaiting me today, I'm visiting the Uyuni Salt Flats.

It's early when we get to the airport, the moon still visible in the sky although it's now light outside. I see the Illimani mountains in the distance, always snow peaked regardless of the time of year but this morning a warm pale pink colour with a white topping, looking just like soft meringue.

The flight is quick and before I know it, I'm greeted by my guide and driver for the coming two days, Israel and Gustavo. With just enough time to collect the wherewithal for our lunch and a quick loo visit, we're off in our gleaming silver four by four.

Our first stop is at the train cemetery; it looks like a railway scrapyard in the middle of a barren, desert like area, the various bits of metal debris have rusted but I'm fascinated by the way the parts create shadows on the light-coloured ground. I click away taking photos of the engines which still look majestic despite their obvious abandonment.

A railway line traverses the wide, flat, open space and continues as far as the eye can see. Israel explains it was built to transport silver from the Bolivian mines to Chile in the late nineteenth century but, with the advent of diesel, the line became defunct, and the trains left to disintegrate here. The remains of this once thriving and lucrative industry give the deserted site a ghost town feel. I can picture a poncho clad Clint Eastwood stepping out from behind one of the engines, cigar in mouth, cowboy hat pulled down over his eyes, holster slung low on his hips, and The Good, The Bad and The Ugly playing in the background.

We set off again and before long the white landscape of the Uyuni Salt Flats, the largest in the world, loom ahead then completely surround us as we venture further into them. I'm shown a block of salt which has been carved out and learn how the markings are like the rings of a tree, each line representing one year. The salt flats occupy over ten thousand square kilometres, a vast space of whiteness, although in the odd area there are pools of water bubbling away, caused by the presence of sulphur.

We stop at Incahuasi, a large mound with distinct species of cacti growing on it. The area used to be under water until a volcano erupted; you can still see the black and pink basalt, and petrified coral in the rocks. Gustavo sets up lunch while Israel and I take a stroll around the mound before joining him; the reflection on the white surface makes the sun very strong and I'm grateful for the canopy which has been erected over our table. There is a tasty, packed lunch to help myself to with water and a large bottle of cocoa cola to drink. I'm also offered red wine, but I turn it down, somehow the surroundings don't go hand in hand with a classy glass of malbec. A number of jeeps are parked up as well but the area is such that they're barely noticeable amongst the vast landscape.

As we head on our way after lunch I notice the odd cloud in the sky, its reflection creating a perfect mirror image in the occasional pools of water I see lying on the expanse of salt. Despite the sameness of the scenery, it's still a glorious sight.

Later we stop again; I've seen the odd hill in the distance but mostly nothing on the horizon except flat whiteness and a brilliant sky. 'Do you like Star Wars?' Israel asks me. 'Some of The Last Jedi was filmed here.' He opens the back of the jeep and takes out a Darth Vada and Stormtrooper toy figure as well as an empty wine bottle. At this point, I have no idea why.

He proceeds to lie flat on the ground on his stomach with Stormtrooper in hand and directs me rather like making a film. 'Keep walking away from me until I tell you to stop.' I do as I'm told, wondering what on earth he has in mind. 'Stop,' he calls out after I'm about thirty metres away. 'Now turn sideways on and put your hands up.' I do as he says and still lying on the ground he takes a photo. 'Come and have a look,' he announces. I return to where he is now standing up and look at the camera image. In it, the thirty-centimetre figure is towering over me; the lack of horizon makes perspective play tricks on what one sees. We do the same with the Darth Vader figure; this time I pretend I'm fighting him with a light sabre in my hand.

'Now let's try something different with the bottle,' Israel announces. Again, he directs me. I look at a different picture this time when he has finished; it appears as if I'm walking on the bottle laying on its side. We finish with another but this time I'm near the camera and the jeep is in the background some one hundred metres away. In the photo I'm pushing a dinky toy version of our vehicle. Israel's certainly going out of his way to make this trip fun.

We arrive at our hotel for the night in plenty of time before the sun goes down. Practically everything it would seem in the Luna Salada Hotel de Sal is made of salt blocks, the walls, pillars, tables, and chairs, even the base of my bed. Israel warns me, 'The heating and hot water are only on for three hours until nine o'clock in the evening and it is very cold in the morning. It is a good idea to have your shower tonight and soon before other guests arrive, otherwise there will not be enough hot water for you.' I'm not looking forward to getting up tomorrow.

Internet access is sketchy and only available in the hotel reception area. Everyone is gathered there by the time I've had my shower, and access is slow. I eventually manage to upload photos and comments on my WhatsApp group chat and also check my messages. Connection with loved ones at home is even more comforting when you're travelling solo.

Israel suddenly appears. 'Would you like to watch the sunset?' He asks. I accept and he goes to fetch Gustavo. 'We will have a better view if we take a short drive,' he explains.

The five-minute journey takes us to an isolated spot where we see the sun is beginning to set. The darkening blue grey sky has thin silver lines of cloud across its expanse, and this time it is the sun's reflection which I can see in the odd pool of water, making it appear as if there are two suns instead of one. Whilst it may not be the most colourful sunset, it's still beautiful, the stillness and total silence around us making the sight even more memorable.

We return to the hotel and go straight into dinner. Gustavo and Israel order a coke and an orange Tango; they seem to be the go-to drinks here, looking around at the other tables. I stick with water. There is a bar area, but everyone retreats to their room after dinner, I'm guessing before the power goes off for the night.

I'm tired, despite having sat in the jeep for the majority of the day, but the sun has been enervating, and it was an early start. I set up my borrowed small camping headlight and strap it round my water bottle, as I'd been advised before I left home; the last thing I want to happen, if the loo calls during the night, is to trip over something. I climb into bed just before the hotel power source goes off, plunging the room into ink black darkness.

The next morning is a six-thirty departure; I wheel my suitcase outside to find Gustavo standing by the jeep, its engine already running. I can hear the heating on and hot air being blasted out, in anticipation of our departure.

We leave the salt flats behind, the terrain changing from flat and white to more a varied landscape now. The wind is strong as is the sun, and we make the odd stop for me to take photos of the rock formations we pass against a backdrop of desert like landscape. The structures are made of volcanic rock; erosion by the wind has resulted in them being formed into unusual shapes, and I'm told this area too was used for scenes in Stars Wars films. I can understand why.

Our first real stop is at the Hedionda Laguna, translated as the Stinky Lagoon, because of the presence of sulphur in the water. Flamingos live here for much of the year, but rather than the bright pink colour one normally associates with them, these birds by contrast are an insipid flesh/whitish colour, due to the lack of algae on which they feed.

When we stop for lunch, Israel takes me on a stroll to look at some pre-Incan ruins nearby. The original town was razed by the Chileans during the Pacific War in the late nineteenth century, then a new town built to replace it lower down the valley. I think what a shame it was not to renovate the old buildings, many of which still exist.

Quinoa with everything is served for lunch; soup with quinoa balls floating in it, then to accompany the main meal, we have quinoa instead of rice or potatoes, and it is also in the dessert, something similar to rice pudding. So far on this trip I've been served quinoa juice and quinoa cakes as well, I even saw an advert, 'Hay cerveza de quinoa'. That's right, a beer made from it.

At one stage on our drive, I see llamas feasting on quinoa husks left over from harvesting. As a food, it's low in calories, high in fibre and protein, and Bolivia has the second highest production in the world behind Peru, although I'm assured by my guide, there are more varieties in his country than anywhere else.

To enable Israel to stock up on his personal supply of cocoa leaves, the jeep takes a slight detour to a hut standing alone, high up at four thousand two hundred metres, almost the highest I've been on the trip. When he comes back out from the remote store, having made his purchase, he kindly offers me a handful. Although my Diamox seems to have done the trick in helping me combat altitude sickness, I accept some as a precautionary measure, and place a few leaves in the corner of my mouth as I was instructed by my Lima guide.

For my final night in Bolivia, I'm staying at the Desert Hotel; the scenery is beautiful, a wide-open area of sand filled landscape with mountains in the background. The sky again is an intense blue with long billowing clouds which, because of the altitude, look close enough to reach out and touch. I think how lucky I've been with the weather; my only rainy day in the two or so weeks since I left home was in La Paz. Despite daily slathering on the sunscreen, my nose has started to peel.

The next day starts with a visit to the red lagoon and it turns out to be the most memorable sight of my trip so far; the deep pinkish maroon water with swathes of white through it and the patches of blue in parts, caused by the reflection of the sky, look unreal, surreal even. The red is caused by microorganisms evidently and I've never seen anything quite so unusual. Think a bowl of borscht with a swirl of cream. The lake is almost deserted because of the early hour; there is just one other vehicle. Despite a drop in temperature caused by a strong wind, I want to take my time here. The spectacle is so strange to my eyes, I feel like I'm on another planet.

Afterwards we move onto the hot springs at Polques. It reminds me of a day trip I took some years ago to Iceland. Yes, I really do mean a day trip. There, I swam in the Blue Lagoon, its milky blue waters vividly contrastingly with the black volcanic rock. I would love to take a dip in the thermal waters here but the wind by now has made the chill factor much colder and the place unsurprisingly is deserted.

It's time to say goodbye and part company with Israel, my guide. He's going to accompany another couple back to Uyuni, and Gustavo will take me on to the border, but, before then, he and I still have a distance to travel. We drive through the Dali Desert, renamed by the locals because the intermittent rocks scattered amongst the desert like terrain make it reminiscent of Salvador Dali paintings. The landscape is spectacular; it reminds me of those bottles you could buy at the seaside, the ones filled with different coloured layers of sand. The shades of cream, ochre, rust, and umber here have to be seen to be believed.

To end my visit to this surprisingly beautiful country, we stop and take in the view of the green and white lagoons. They sit literally side by side with nothing between them, the white one coloured by borax and the green by arsenic. Unsurprisingly the green one has no living creature in or on it, contrastingly the white one does. Their physical closeness to each other is uncanny with only a narrow bank separating the water, another reminder of how amazing planet Earth is.

The guard is having his lunch when we arrive and get out of the car at the Bolivian border, he barely stops eating to take a cursory glance at my passport, before nonchalantly stamping it and returning to his food, as if that's far more important to him. I'm not surprised by his laidback approach; it somehow fits with what I've seen of the country's culture in my short visit. I thank Gustavo profusely for his kindness and he checks again I have no food with me; it's illegal to bring any foodstuffs into Chile. I climb on board a large minibus, the only occupant bar the driver, to take me to the Chilean passport control and onward to my next country.

And so, I say goodbye to Bolivia with its generally low standard of hotels, unmade roads, continually high altitude, often over four thousand metres, (thank goodness for Diamox and cocoa leaves), extremes of temperature from day to night and poor WIFI. But what a beautiful country. If you ever visit, you won't be disappointed with the views. Venga a Bolivia!

At the Bolivian border

Moon Valley

Train cemetery at Uyuni

The vast expanse of the Uyuni Salt Flats

Held to ransom by a thirty centimetre stormtrooper

Chile

After a short drive through treeless rolling hills to the Chilean border, I see a single industrial unit in front of us. 'We wait here,' my driver says to me, his lone passenger. Five minutes later we're still waiting. Unlike the informality of the Bolivian border, there is a sense of foreboding here; the austere building with its tall roller door rather like a loading bay, remains shut with no-one in sight. My driver does another check with me. 'You must not have food with you,' he reminds me. I've already jettisoned the few boiled sweets I usually carry with me and shake my head.

Eventually I hear the mechanism being operated and see the door slowly being raised, rather like a curtain in the theatre at the start of a tense drama. However, there is still no person to be seen, the set is bare. We drive in and I'm instructed by my driver to get out of the bus and wait. He proceeds to take my case and lay it on a long metal table. I look up the steps in front of me to see an armed guard patrolling at the top, his rifle positioned across his chest, while another descends the stairs and instructs me to open my luggage. I do as he says then nonchalantly put my hands in my pockets, trying to look confident. I don't know why I feel the need to do so but am finding the whole scenario intimidating. It is then that my hand rests on the cocoa leaves in my pocket, the ones Israel had given me to help with the altitude. I freeze. Would the leaves count as foodstuffs; in theory they aren't as one wouldn't eat them, or are they? What should I do, confess and take the risk of I don't know what, or keep stumm and hope I'm not searched? I decide to keep quiet.

The contents of my case are given a brief once over before the guard nods his head in the direction of a particular door, indicating for me to go through it. My heart is thumping, wondering what might lie beyond it, a body search maybe or a sniffer dog? I'm somewhat relieved to see a friendlier face sat behind a desk with passport stamp in hand. Soon I'm back on the bus and we're through the border crossing. I give out a sigh of relief but don't completely relax until several miles later. So much for my triple checking everything motto.

Looking back at the incident later, I don't know why I was so nervous, after all is it likely a seventy-year-old would be arrested for a few cocoa leaves? But then one never knows.

The accommodation at San Pedro de Atacama consists of small chalets rather than rooms, and looks like a haven compared to my hotels in Bolivia. I have a spacious room with a, could easily sleep three people, bed and a small sofa, the brightly coloured cushions casually scattered adding to the ethnic feel. I immediately make use of the walk-in shower and toiletries on offer then wrap myself in a voluminous white fluffy towelling robe.

I suddenly remember I haven't done any laundry for six days and had planned to make it a priority on my arrival here. I'm in San Pedro for two nights and estimate that should be enough time to get things dry. A word about my packing habits here, I have four criteria for what to take with me wherever possible; one-light to pack, two-fabric which doesn't crease much, three-doesn't take up much room in my case, and four- can be washed and dried overnight. Of course it can't apply to everything I take, fleeces have been much needed on this trip, but clothing which fits my criteria make the ideal travelling companion.

I quickly get the washing done and then open a door leading to my outside area; bamboo screens enclose it, offering me privacy should I want to make use of my outdoor shower some time. The heat immediately hits me; the Atacama Desert is one of the driest places on earth, with low humidity. I put my washing to dry, hanging some over the shower head and other bits on a deckchair, then sit in the other one, feeling the warmth of the sun on my face and enjoying the chance to relax. The constant early starts to my day on this trip are catching up with me, even though much of my time has been spent sitting in a car and being driven, however, I haven't had a completely free day since Cusco, eight days earlier.

I awake with a jolt an hour later and realise I'd dozed off, not a clever idea in this heat and without sunscreen on. To my amazement and delight, in that short time, all my washing is already bone dry.

My reason for being here is to visit the Tatio Geysers, best seen early in the morning as the sun is rising. I'm collected by minibus at four thirty the next morning, then transferred to a coach where a number of other tourists are waiting. It is minus thirteen degrees Celsius outside and to add to the cold, the heater in the bus isn't working. Although I'm wearing my warmest clothes, including thermals, I'm freezing by the time we get there.

It's still dark although a patch of sky is beginning to show signs of getting lighter. I stamp my feet, trying to get some feeling back into them as we're led by our guide from the coach to where there are the first signs of what look like puffs of smoke being emitted from the ground. Gradually more appear, only now, as it gets lighter, I can see they aren't smoke but columns of water and steam. Perhaps my lack of enthusiasm is to do with how cold I'm feeling but the ones here don't begin to compare to Rotorua in New Zealand or is it that when your whole body feels like a block of ice it's difficult to enjoy anything. Whatever the reason, Tatio isn't holding the same interest as its New Zealand counterpart, with the close links it has there to the Māori heritage.

I give up following the guide and return to where the coach driver is setting up a table with an urn and snacks on. Two cups of coffee later, when the rest of the group join us, I'm still trying get some sensation in my feet and hands.

On the way back to the coach later, we walk by the thermal springs where a number of people in swim gear are enjoying the steaming water. I shiver at the sight. Better men (and women) than I am Gunga Din!

We pass through desert landscape on our fifty-mile journey back to San Pedro de Atacama but make a stop on the way. By now the sun has begun to creep higher in the clear blue sky but it's still not hot enough for me to consider removing any layers of clothing. There is a queue forming outside one of the low buildings and I go over to investigate. Three tourists whom I'd noticed on my coach explain to me, 'Everyone's waiting to buy food.' I realise I too am hungry and join them to wait our turn.

'Are you on holiday?' I ask.

One of them replies in an Australian accent, 'Yes,' and points to himself and one of the women, who turns out to be his wife.

'And no,' the other woman replies, in a perfect English accent.

'Oh, you're British,' I comment.

'Yes and no.' The three of them laugh at my confusion. 'Born in Brazil of English parents so dual nationality, went to school in Scotland but now living in Chile.' I join in the laughter, trying to get my head round this woman's heritage.

By now we've reached the front of the queue, I look at the board above the counter and see what's on offer; the choice is sparse. I, like my companions, buy the only two things on the menu then make my way outside again to enjoy the increasing warmth of the sun. I'm relieved when I can begin to feel my feet and hands at last. I tuck into my purchases, warm, cheese empanadas and llama kebabs, both of which taste delicious. The guide comes over and tells us llamas have very little fat, like ostrich. I glance across the road to see a few of the said animals in an enclosure, but don't feel in the slightest bit guilty as I savour the tasty meat.

'Would you like to join us for coffee?' The English/Brazilian, educated in Scotland, now living in Chile, woman asks, when we reach San Pedro. It turns out the Aussie man is a cousin of the English/Brazilian, educated in Scotland woman, and he and his wife have been staying with her. I order a beer when the server comes to take our order, causing him to say something in Spanish, however I only catch part of it. The English/Brazilian woman explains, 'It's not possible to order a drink without food, evidently it's the law in San Pedro.' So, we settle on a plate of chips to share; certainly not a hardship for me, they were delicious washed down with the local beer.

It transpires the English/Brazilian woman and I, by coincidence, did our teacher training at the same institution and she is moving to England permanently the following year. We swap contact details before I leave them, should we want to meet up when she has settled in England.

The town is clearly popular with tourists, and I decide to have a wander round before returning to my hotel. I like the atmosphere of the place, it has a casual, laid-back feel. There are cafes with the delicious sounding eggs rancheros on their menus, houses offering cheap laundry services and hiking shops selling a wide array of equipment and clothing. I browse in a few shops and buy a Patagonia long sleeved T-shirt to take back for my son out law, (thus named because he and my daughter are partners but not married), I then seek out a grocery store to replenish my snack collection; crackers, a couple of energy bars, and some boiled sweets, the likes of which I had to throw away at the border.

The next morning, I leave the haven of San Pedro after just forty hours to catch my flight onwards, across the Andes to reach my next destination, the capital, Santiago.

My hotel is in a bustling area of the city. The road outside has a wide pedestrian path down its centre, a large, beautiful, ornate fountain and is canopied by trees, giving it the same feel as the long boulevards in France or Spanish avenidas. In fact, I can already see that much of the city's architecture seems to be heavily influenced by the Spanish. I notice the well patronised cycleways at the side of roads are separated from the rest of the traffic by concrete humps about fifty centimetres high. A great idea; no chance for either cycle or car to veer into each other's lanes here.

My hotel has an attractive art deco entrance with colourful blue and yellow leaded glass doors, while the lift to the rooms is one of the old-fashioned types with a concertina metal door which one has to close manually before the lift will move, giving the whole place a stylish retro feel. My room is small but adequate, the king size bed taking up much of the space; on the bedside table is a small box of chocolates and the complimentary toiletries smell classy, just like everything else I've seen so far in this hotel.

I decide to eat in the rooftop hotel restaurant this evening; the tapas menu sounds tempting; however, I go for the suckling pig ribs instead, which turn out to be an excellent choice. I hungrily devour them and then sit sucking the sticky sauce from my fingers while I gaze in wonderment at the blood red sky, a glass of Chilean cabernet at hand, waiting for my attention.

My itinerary says a winery tour in the morning and then a city tour in the afternoon. I think what an odd way round that is but go with the flow anyway. A minibus collects me and takes me to a central gathering place where my fellow passengers and I are directed into other minibuses, each one going to a different winery; mine is Undurraga, one I've heard of but know nothing about. I'm pleased to discover I have a private tour and therefore a guide to myself. Now there are pros and cons to this; on the one hand you aren't hanging around waiting for others and you also have the guide's undivided attention, meaning you can ask as many questions as you like. On the other hand, in a group situation, the experience is shared and when one is travelling alone, sometimes it can be a pleasant change to be with others.

I learn about the wine making process as we wander among the rows of vines and notice there is a single rose bush planted at the end of each one. My guide explains, 'This is a way of detecting the onset of disease. If the roses show signs of it, then the leaves will be analysed and treated before deciding how to treat the vines.' Clever or what?

We venture inside to the Aroma Room where I'm left to walk round in my own time. Along every wall is a chest high shelf with a row of large glass receptacles sitting on them.

Each one emits a certain smell which can be found in wine, from cut hay to wet earth to chocolate or toast plus a whole load of others. I'm intrigued by the number and variety of aromas I breathe in; it reminds me of the perfume exhibition at Somerset House in London. The multitude of different scents there was just as surprising.

I emerge from inside and come out into an area with vintage carriages on display. There are other people round and about, all of us waiting for the tastings to begin, tables have been laid out for each group with bottles on them, ready to be tried. I'm delighted to be the only one standing in front of my table, another advantage of a private tour.

We start with a Riesling, one of my favourites; it is light, buttery, and very drinkable. Next, my guide introduces me to a wine only produced in Chile, carmenere. (I'd never heard of it before). Lighter than a cabernet sauvignon but with more depth than a merlot, it tastes slightly sharp. I wonder what sort of food it would go well with but don't ask this time because we're swiftly moving on to the Undurraga cabernet sauvignon, a full-bodied wine but without the strong tannin taste of a malbec. The tasting finishes with a dessert wine. Delish! Being the sole person on this particular tour has its advantages as far as the tasting is concerned, the samples were certainly more than generous, although I'm mindful of the fact that I have the city tour in the afternoon. Nevertheless, I do try a little more of the Riesling.

The city tour, this time as part of a group, is pleasant enough; we see significant buildings and churches galore, and I'm also pleased the flamingos in City Park look more in the pink than those in Bolivia. Many of the trees are decorated with giant pink bows; I ask my guide of their significance, wondering if it's breast cancer awareness month here in Chile, but he doesn't know.

By the time we've finished for the day, I'm hungry, having only had a muffin and a banana secreted from breakfast for my lunch. I ask at my hotel for a good place to eat and am directed to the Bellavista area a five-minute walk away, where there are a number of eateries to choose from.

I browse in one of the jewellery shops in the same complex as the restaurants and notice a silver pendant with a diamond shaped red stone. The colour is so unusual that I'm immediately drawn to it, however, sense prevails when I remember I have no earrings to match. Unless……! The salesperson returns it to the display cabinet when I shrug my shoulders and exit the shop; I really like the pendant but am also aware I still have four weeks of my trip to go and a budget to be mindful of. My reason goes out of the window a few minutes later when I look in another shop and see a pair of silver earrings also with a red inlay. Although not the same diamond shape, the colour would match perfectly. I'm in a dilemma and change my mind several times while I wander around looking at the menus displayed outside the various restaurants. Part of me is thinking, I'll probably not see anything like this again, and another part is saying, 'Be sensible Jan, you still have many more days to go on this trip.' My mind is made up when I spy a shop, rather like a MacDonalds, selling only a selection of hot dogs and fries. A good compromise I think, a cheap as chips meal, if you'll excuse the pun, and I could get both the earrings and pendant. I choose a hot dog with avocado, tomatoes and mayonnaise, called an Italiano completo because of the similarity in colour to the green, red, and white flag of Italy. It's delicious. With my little bags of jewellery tucked away in my suitcase and a satisfied stomach, I go to bed that night feeling very happy.

Valparaiso is a city seventy miles or so from Santiago, a popular stop for cruise liners and a busy port for container shipping. And today it's where my itinerary takes me. Our coach drops us off at Alegre Hill, one of two hills given status as a UNESCO world heritage site. I can see hostels, cafes, and bars juxtaposed with grand old houses which have been left to go to wrack and ruin. This was once an area of wealth until the Panama Canal was built and trade to and from the Atlantic and Pacific Oceans via Valparaiso was severely affected as ships chose to take the quicker route rather than via the Straits of Magellan.

The surroundings at first glance look on the unkempt, shabby side, however, when I take the time to look beyond the rundown buildings, I begin to appreciate the beauty of what was a chic residential area, built on the side of a hill. The community now has its own unique identity, certainly different from before I would imagine; the abundance of murals which decorate the walls and doors add colour and style. Our guide explains painting has been encouraged by the local municipality in order to obliterate tagging, and the murals have now become part of the character of the area, adding to its Bohemian feel. There are plans afoot to renovate the decaying grand houses, by turning them into boutique hotels and cultural centres. The place seems to hold the same charm as I remember Montmartre did in the 1960s, also Santa Christina in Rio de Janeiro.

We follow the street and snake our way down the hill on foot before the guide brings us to a halt halfway. 'Anybody want to try a different way of getting down?' He asks, pointing to a ten-metre-long slide connecting where we're standing with the street below. I hear gasps of surprise behind me and kindly laughter when I'm the first to sit on and I allow the slide to descend me. I may be considerably older than my fellow tourists, and this behaviour from a septuagenarian is not what they expect, but I'm up for it. Our descent is concluded by a ride on a funicular to take us to where our coach is waiting. I make a mental note; two more modes of transport to add to my list.

When I return to my hotel later, I chuckle to myself at how others in the group had reacted at the sight of me careering down on the slide, and I conclude I've served my generation well today. There's something satisfying about challenging assumptions with regard to older people. However, I don't let my mind dwell on it for long; there are plenty more adventures still to come because the next day I'll be moving onto my next stayover, somewhere it isn't possible to travel to by road, slide, or funicular. I'm catching a flight to Easter Island.

Santiago airport is buzzing despite the early hour, and I have a slight panic when I'm told at check in, I should have filled in some sort of entry form to accompany my passport. I follow directions to another part of the terminal and find an innocuous looking desk surrounded by it would seem, travellers like me who were unaware of this entry requirement. Bags come unzipped and sheets of paper with my itinerary are rifled through as I search for the address of my hotel on the Isla de Pasqual, which I can't find anywhere among the information I've been given. I manage to get the attention of the woman behind the desk, point to the spot on the form and shrug my shoulders. She shrugs her shoulders in return and mutters something, then shoos me on to make room for other passengers waiting to complete the paperwork. I take out my mobile, log on to the airport Wi-Fi and after much sifting and sorting, eventually find what I hope is the address. Phew! Not a great problem but something I wasn't expecting. Judging by the number of people at the same desk, neither were they.

The wait in the departure lounge isn't a long one before my flight is called. I take my time, never seeing the point in rushing to get on the plane, sitting in a cramped space with someone's elbow taking up the armrest you're supposed to be sharing, so I wait until most people have boarded before I join the by now dwindling line. The cabin steward greets me. 'Welcome onboard,' and indicates with her left arm for me to go into the cabin on my right. I look at the numbers written on the overhead lockers to indicate which seat I'm in but can't fathom it. I look at the next row which is fully occupied by now but still can't see my seat number. The cabin steward comes to help me, gives out an 'Ah,' and uses her right arm this time to direct me into the correct cabin. Somehow, I've been upgraded to business class (I know not why). The seats are so spacious that I won't be needing to share an armrest, in fact the seat beside me is unoccupied. Whoopee! For the five-hour flight, I can spread out as much as I like.

I've missed out on the first round of champagne but as soon as we're airborne, I'm brought a choice of either orange juice or champagne. I decide on both; what better way to start off than with a buck's fizz. Soon I'm tucking into my second breakfast of the day; muesli and yogurt, warm bread with conserves, orange juice, and coffee.

The hotel where I'm staying is about a twenty-minute drive outside the main drag; at first glimpse I can see its position on a hillside affords the most wonderful views over the Pacific Ocean. The elliptical shaped chalets dotted amongst the shrubbery are painted white with contrasting black markings and have wide patio doors. Before unpacking, I slide them open and admire the view. The black rock boulders, which are typical of the island, contrast with the lush greenery, there are a wide range of flame-coloured flowers, a few of which I recognise; pretty, orange hibiscus and red-hot pokers, but many others are unfamiliar. The shimmering sea in the distance makes the perfect backcloth.

Another huge bed awaits me in the centre of my room, only this one is exceptionally low to the ground and there is no bedside table to lean on to help me get up or down. I try the bed and then have to invent an ungainly sideways roll to haul myself up to standing; a sumo wrestler would have been proud of my move. My knees have served me well over the years but pushing up from the low position to standing would be too much to ask of them. I have visions of me sideways rolling out of bed in the middle of the night to have a wee and crawling crablike to the bathroom. At least that way I wouldn't have to be a nuisance to my creaking joints.

The hotel is rather isolated and the only option for eating, other than taking a cab to a busier part of the island, is the hotel restaurant. My eyes open wide when I look at the prices, the cheapest item on the menu is a modest chicken sandwich at twenty-six quid. I know much of the foodstuff for the island has to be imported and had expected to pay more than normal, but the price is exorbitant. In the end, I decide to make do with a can of pop from my stash, a packet of crisps and an energy bar. These and my two breakfasts I'd enjoyed earlier, would have to be enough to see me through till tomorrow. It's not that I'm on a tight budget, I'm more fortunate than many people, but perhaps it's my upbringing which makes me thrifty, a legacy of the way my parents' generation had to manage during and then after the Second World War. Value for money, make do and mend, save the pennies and the pounds will look after themselves, happen to be ways of thinking I grew up with, and in some ways helped to define me.

My three-night stay on Easter Island includes two full day tours, meaning my time is going to be packed with visits to the various sites to see the Moai, the monumental figures, some as tall as twenty metres, which it is thought were carved by Polynesians when they inhabited the island.

Our guide is difficult to understand, he swaps from Portuguese to English at a whim to accommodate the mix of nationalities in the minibus, but his accent is so bad that sometimes I'm not aware when he starts talking in English again, and he also gets tetchy when I ask him for clarification. In the end I resolve to sit back and just enjoy the sights, a shame though, I would have liked to understand more of the island's history and culture.

Throughout the day we visit various locations and see a number of Moai, one with topknot and coral eyes, others in a line at another site, uniform in size and standing like sentries on duty, and seven Moai looking out to sea at a third place. These ones are unique in that, unlike the others on the island, they face with their backs to the ocean.

We stop for lunch before our tour continues, and I join Australians Kerry and Glen, Earl from the US, and Daphna from Greece in a local restaurant. We all opt for fish, although not the same dishes. My meal when it comes is huge and served with two fried eggs on top. I won't need to have dinner in the hotel restaurant tonight for sure.

While we eat, the five of us talk about where else we've visited in Chile, and I enjoy hearing their stories. Daphna is on a two-year long trip around the world and has the smallest of cabin cases for her luggage. Evidently, she carries only one change of clothing. 'I don't need to have much with me,' she explains. 'For me the trip is all about the places I visit and the people I meet, not worrying about what I look like.' She's right, I've found plenty of travellers willing to engage in conversation, meeting those people and the wonderful sights will be the memories I'll hold onto at the end of my adventure.

The next day, I'm disappointed to see I have the same guide. I have a brief chat with Earl, he has requested to change groups, like me he wasn't happy with our guide from the previous day, but by now it's too late for me to do the same. I resign myself to yet another day like yesterday; it's not that it was bad but not as good as I would have liked.

Our first stop is the quarry, where the stone for the Moai was mined and then carved. About half of the total on the island still rest here and today I have the chance to see them up close. Some of the imposing figures stand tall while others rest at an angle in the ground, their dark stone contrasting with the colour of the grass where they sit. We follow a steep, winding pathway walking amongst them, one minute passing close by the gigantic sculptures then dipping down to look back at the them as they now tower over us.

Lunch is included today, referred to in my itinerary as a box lunch, consequently I'm expecting something akin to a packed lunch, maybe a roll and juice, but instead we're taken to an area with a barbeque on the go where chicken and beef steaks are cooking over the hot coals. There are also a number of different salads laid out, ready to choose from. Very tasty and certainly enough that I won't want anything else to eat that evening again.

Our last stop of the day is the beach; it is a Saturday and consequently busy. We pile out of the minibus, my fellow travellers and I, to get the perfect photoshot of the Moai, this time with the shimmering blue of the Pacific in the background. A juice stall has a wide range of freshly made drinks on offer, sounding too good to resist. I sip on my papaya, lime and mango and gaze out to sea; the Pitcairn Islands, the nearest inhabited land to the west, and Australia are many thousands of miles away. Even the mainland of Chile to the east is over two thousand miles from Easter Island.

This evening, I pull open my patio doors and sit and enjoy a spectacular sunset; the sky, punctuated with silvery striated clouds, varies in colour, turning from gold then pale yellow to grey as it gets lower, and then darkening where the horizon meets the sea, making it impossible to fathom where the line between the sky ends and the water begins. This tiny island in the Pacific with its tropical landscape, beautiful scenery, and strange figures which nobody knows for sure who built them or what they represent, is an enigma, yet tourists flock here to experience the place for themselves and to find out more about the mysteries the island holds.

Two days later, I stare out of the plane and see dark imposing looking mountains beneath me and I wonder what southern Chile and Patagonia will have in store. On my return to Santiago, I'd stayed overnight at the airport and then early the next morning, taken the sixth internal flight of my trip to Punta Arenas. I now have a three-hour onward drive to my next destination with, I've been informed, a non-English speaking driver. No doubt we'll muddle through between us with sign language and my pidgin Spanish.

I've read about Patagonia in the book, Between Extremes, written by John McCarthy and Brian Keenan. During the four years they were held hostage in Lebanon, they dreamed of running a llama farm here and used it as a way of distracting themselves from thinking about the possible outcomes of their imprisonment. Then, some years after they were released, they paid the area a visit to see if the reality matched the images they'd conjured up in their mind. As I'm driven, I can see the vast wide-open spaces of the Patagonian landscape against snow-capped mountains, matching the description in the book well. I have to pinch myself when I see signposts to Magellan Strait and Tierra del Fuego, the most southerly area in South America. Memories of those geography lessons come flooding back.

There is a pretty view out of my bedroom window at the hotel where I'm staying in Puerto Natales. It's of the Bay of Esperanza with mountains towering over the body of water. A card on the bedside table advertises the hotel's laundry service; it's very cheap, the equivalent in pesos to four quid for a bagful the size of a pillowcase. Washing and drying clothes when you're constantly changing accommodation can be a problem; I usually avoid the expense of inhouse laundry services when I can, (I make no excuse again for my frugality), but this offer is too good to ignore. Definitely a win, win situation I decide. I rummage through my case, sort out what needs to be done and put it ready to be collected. The front desk assures me it will be returned the following afternoon.

I sit and enjoy my first cup of tea of the trip, apart from mate that is, then take a pleasant forty-five-minute stroll before dinner. My body needs it after two days of mostly travelling, either sitting in a car or on a plane. Trawlers have docked for the night on the edge of the bay, it is dusk and a lovely fresh evening with no wind, an element Patagonia is renowned for. The sunset gives the sky an orange glow behind the mountains, and I think to myself for the umpteenth time how lucky I am to be experiencing this. I'm already on my third country and even by now, the trip has exceeded my expectations.

My pisco sour with boysenberry is a pleasant pre dinner appetiser; I'd never heard of the fruit but when I google it, I find it's a cross between a raspberry, loganberry, and blackberry. I nod to the group of four Australians also sitting in the bar; I recognise them from the flight from Easter Island, and they had also stayed at the same airport hotel in Santiago. After dinner, they call over to me, 'Come and join us for a glass of wine.' Without exception I've found all my fellow travellers throughout the trip to be friendly but the Aussies I've met have gone out of their way to make this 'older' lady feel welcome. I refuse the glass of red wine I've been offered, having already enjoyed a glass of malbec with my meal as well as the pisco sour, but accept the offer to join them. They're embarking on a cruise the next day, one which will take them through the channels and fjords of southern Patagonia. The trip sounds exciting. Oh, to have more time exploring this wondrous continent!

The next morning, there is the palest of blue skies with the moon still visible when I go to breakfast, and a mist is coming off the bay. This soon clears and I'm treated to gorgeous reflections in the water with a now pink glow in the sky and over the mountains as I eat. I take a photo and, on looking at it back, the image seems unreal, as if I've added a pink filter.

The minibus carrying the group I'm in arrives at the entrance to the Torres del Paine National Park and, although cold, there is still no sign of the infamous wind; it looks like

I'm going to be lucky with the weather again. Our guide tells us that sometimes a jaguar can be seen prowling among the rocks in the hillside above us first thing in the morning, but there is no sighting of it today.

The landscape as we drive through the park is dominated by the three distinctive granite peaks, and a popular challenge for hikers; there is the option of the W route (up and down) or O route (around) to explore the towers, both taking days to complete. Rather like the Inca trail, the trek acts as a rite of passage for backpackers, and I can see some of them already at the start, waiting to tackle their chosen route.

Our minibus continues through the park, stopping at various points and giving us the chance to take photos; the reflections of the surrounding mountains and of the now bright blue sky in the glacial lakes are so clear, a mirror image too perfect to look real. We stop to take in another view of the three peaks in the distance but this time there is a herd of guanacos grazing in the foreground. Mother nature at its absolute best; what an environment to live in.

We stop for lunch then sway our way across the swing bridge to see Lake Grey. It is relatively empty of water still, too early in spring for the glaciers to have begun to melt yet and for the water to make its journey down to flow into it. We do catch sight of a few small pale aqua icebergs in the lake though, standing isolated at the moment, and waiting to be engulfed by the ice-cold water from the mountainside as the temperature rises.

Words can't begin to describe the beauty of Torres del Paine; the majestic mountains, the glaciers, the clear mirror like lakes, and today all against a background of a cerulean sky. Wherever one looks there are chocolate box views. In the end I put my camera away and take the time to enjoy just being here. What a spectacle!

The hotel receptionist is curious about my itinerary when I settle my bill that evening and explain tomorrow will be my last day in Chile. She asks me, 'Did you visit the Lake District while you were here?' I shake my head apologetically. There is so much to see in this long narrow country, bordered completely on one side by the Pacific Ocean and on the other by a chain of mountain ranges. It is full of contrasts, from the dryness of the Atacama Desert to the hustle and bustle of Santiago and the multitude of wineries nearby, the arty decadence of Valparaiso, the mysticism of Easter Island and the spectacular scenery of Torres del Paine. Another time, another trip maybe, but for me, today is the end of my Chilean road, because tomorrow I take the tourist bus across the border into Argentina. Always another adventure around the corner if you're willing to take the chance.

Cheese empanadas in the Atacama Desert

Valparaiso

The beautiful Torres Del Paine National Park

Esperanza Bay at dusk, like a Jack Vettriano painting

Argentina

My guide checks me in at the bus station and shows me which coach to board, she makes sure my suitcase is stored away and finds where I'm sitting. I'm glad to discover the tourist bus is clean, spacious, and comfortable; a reclining seat awaits me, there is a loo on board, only a handful of passengers and we have two drivers who will take it in turns to do the driving. Any concerns I have about travelling this part of the trip are dissipating.

It takes an hour to reach the Chilean border; we all get off the coach and stand in line to have our passports checked. The extra coach driver is very helpful and waits with us ready to deal with any queries which may arise, but there are no problems, and within twenty minutes we're all back on the bus. We go through the same routine at the Argentina border control; there is no need to lug my suitcase off for a luggage check and again the procedure is straightforward. My worries beforehand are proving to be totally unfounded.

By mid afternoon I've been met at the bus station and dropped off at my hotel in El Calafate. I unpack for my two nights stay then decide to have a mosey around. Similar to countries like India, it isn't possible to buy currency outside of Argentina, consequently I sort out how many Argentine pesos I think I'll need and look for a money exchange shop.

Rather like San Pedro de Atacama, the town has a backpacker feel although the prices on the restaurant menus, as I wander around, indicate otherwise. I know Patagonia is similar to Easter Island in that respect, both areas needing to import many of their commodities, making the price of foodstuffs higher.

I decide to eat in the hotel restaurant in the evening until that is, I ask for tap water to drink. Now I should explain, I have a bee in my bonnet about places where only bottled water is served, some are understandable, for example where the water isn't treated, but I take umbrage at having to pay for water. I'm in two minds, part of me is thinking, don't be such a scrooge, and the other part is saying, stick to your principles. The server looks at me in amazement when I get up to leave. I go in search of a shop to buy a few nibbles and fruit to get me by, they'll have to do until breakfast tomorrow.

After a good eight hours sleep, I'm ready to visit Los Glaciares National Park the next day; nothing in my wildest imagination would prepare my eyes for what they were about to see. I'm still getting over the beauty of Torres del Paine and haven't come down to earth from that spectacle, and then we arrive at the Perito Moreno Glacier. Bigger than the whole of Buenos Aires, it is part of the southern Patagonia Icefield; seventy kilometres long and two hundred and sixty-four square kilometres in area, the third largest glacier on the planet, and the largest outside of Antarctica. My only sighting of glaciers before today has been in two places; Torres del Paine yesterday, where they had sat snugly at an angle on the mountainside, waiting to be melted then tipping their water to top up the mirror like lakes below, and Queensland in New Zealand, where I took a helicopter trip to land on one. Here in Los Glaciares, the experience is totally different.

I hop on a boat with ninety odd other passengers to take a closer look. From a distance, the glacier looks a little like the white cliffs of Dover, an expanse of white and pale grey forming a backdrop against the sea, but as we get closer the colour changes to the lightest of blue. I've decided to stand on the upper deck, uncovered except for the canvas canopy over part of it. It's windy and cold but this way I don't have to share the view with so many people, and I'm determined not to miss a moment. The colours and hues change by the minute, in one place the palest of milky blue and in another, a deep cobalt. Every now and then you hear a cracking sound as huge chunks of the glacier break off and crash down, shooting the water around it high into the air. Our boat keeps a respectful distance. The odd masses of ice in the water, bits of the glacier which have broken off, are more turquoise in colour and contrast sharply with the dull grey of the water. The sky is overcast today and bereft of blue, but the lack of it allows instead the colours in the glacier to take centre stage. A jaw dropping moment; the sheer size, the colour and beauty of it is something very special.

Later we're dropped off at the viewpoint overlooking the glacier; here I can get a closer view of its structure. The colour gets more intense the deeper the crevices get, and the sharp points look like the Needles on the Isle of Wight, although these ones are packed tighter together to create a solid mass, and there are many more of them. I've been lucky to see many special sights on my trip, but this one brings a tear to my eye. The wonder of the natural world takes your breath away at times; images of today will stay with me forever.

While I wait in the hotel reception for my cab to take me to the airport the next day, I get chatting to an English couple who are going to hike across the glacier today. Now that's another experience I would like to have tried. However, I have another place to be, in the words of the song from Evita, 'What's new Buenos Aires?'

My hotel is in a suburb called Recoleta, in the northern part of the city, and well known because of the cemetery of the same name, where Eva Peron's family vault lies. I decide to take a look round there; it's only a two-minute walk away and easy to find with a grand gated entrance. Outside, a couple dance the Argentine tango while onlookers watch, one even asks if she can be taught, for a tip of course. The male dancer takes her by the hand and holding her close around the waist, guides her through some of the movements. Even with a novice the dance looks intimate, sultry even, and it sets the mood perfectly for what I anticipate will be an exciting and fascinating part of my trip in a couple of days time.

Recoleta cemetery contains nearly five thousand mausoleums, its narrow 'streets' giving it the feel of a model village for the dead. In terms of austerity, it has a sense of foreboding rather than the peace and calm I usually associate with cemeteries. The tall vaults and their proximity to one another make them appear intimidating, some have stairs leading down to an underground vault while others are above ground with highly embellished frontages. It feels strange walking around and a little spooky, as if I'm on a film set and an actor dressed as a zombie is going to suddenly emerge from behind one of the tall stone crosses.

I happen across the vault of the Duarte family, adorned with flowers. People still leave floral tributes here to celebrate the life of the family's most famous member. Eva Peron died in the nineteen fifties of cancer, however, when General Juan Peron was overthrown and banished, the body of his wife was moved to Italy to prevent its presence being used to incite another coup. It wasn't till Peron was allowed to return to his home country, nearly twenty years later, that Eva's body could be interred in the family vault.

I've decided to treat myself and have dinner in the hotel restaurant this evening. It's more upmarket than most of the places I've been staying in but I'm in the mood for a touch of spoilaciousness and the menu looks enticing. The rack of lamb with fondant potatoes and roasted veg, accompanied by a glass of cabernet sauvignon from Mendoza is deliciously tasty, and despite there being only a handful of diners in the restaurant, I still enjoy the ambience. I'm just finishing off my wine when a couple enter the restaurant and approach me. We'd met a few weeks before in Santiago and I remember the man telling me at the time how much he was looking forward to Easter Island. Like me, he'd harboured a dream of coming to South America since he was a child, reading about and being particularly fascinated by Easter Island's history. I ask him if his trip there lived up to expectations. His face lights up and I could tell straightaway he hadn't been disappointed. He talks about the spirituality he felt at the quarry, as if the ghosts of its ancestors were still present.

The couple also mention the riots which had taken place in Santiago a couple of weeks after I left and the curfew put in place. They, like me, had just missed the political unrest, but some tourists had been waiting to hear if it was safe for them to continue with their itinerary. Thank goodness I'd already done that part of my trip before it all kicked off, however it does make me realise how precarious my plans might have been.

My city tour the following morning is in a small group and I'm pleased to say the guide is easy to understand, swapping between English and Portuguese to accommodate all his passengers. The temperature has noticeably increased, and my shorts, T-shirt and sandals are on at last. How good it is to feel the sun on my back after having spent several days in the Patagonia climate.

Our first stop is the Casa Rosada, where Eva Peron delivered her famous speech, and the setting for the Evita song, *Don't Cry for Me Argentina*. I wish I could have stayed longer in the square, to take my time imagining what it would have been like to stand among the crowds and hear her rallying the people, but our attention is diverted in the direction of the Metropolitan Cathedral across the way where Pope Francis, the first pope from South America to hold the position, used to lead mass.

And then we're back in the minibus to move on to our next sight. We pass a gigantic twenty-metre-high flower sculpture mass of steel and aluminium in one of the many parks; the flower opens and closes at the beginning and end of each day and is controlled by hydraulic and photoelectric sensors. It glimmers in the bright sun. Later we come to Ninth Avenue, with its eleven lanes and a total of one hundred and forty-three metres wide, considered the widest thoroughfare in the world. We're understandably wary of traffic as we walk across and of cars starting up before we've reached the other side. However, we survive unscathed.

La Boca area near the docks has a sense of arty playfulness about it but at one time was a notoriously dangerous area where immigrants would arrive from different parts of the world to find employment and a better life. I'd been told beforehand by one of my work colleagues there is a large Welsh community still living in the city, descendants of families who had done just that and then settled here.

Workers off the ships would also come ashore to find their entertainment in La Boca, and prostitutes would ply their trade, and of course it was where the Argentine tango was created in the bars and brothels. Now the area is a tourist attraction. There are colourfully painted houses with walls made of corrugated iron; it was a cheap commodity when they were built, even the public loo is multicoloured (and very clean), and there is an abundance of street art. Along Caminto, artisans display their wares and life sized figures sit on balconies above, with hands aloft as if waving to you, giving the street a quirky feel.

Our tour includes a visit to Recoleta cemetery, the second one for me. There is a ceremony taking place in front of one of the vaults when we arrive. It just so happens our visit coincides with the anniversary of General Roca's death, an ex-president of Argentina. There is a military presence with a dozen soldiers in ceremonial dress from, I'm told, the Patricios regiment, the oldest unit of the Argentine army. Their navy-blue jackets with bright red sashes and white trousers contrast sharply with the grey and black of the surroundings, and their highly polished boots make a rhythmic sound as they march, accompanied by the clink and rattle of their swords.

I'm back at my hotel by mid afternoon, giving me a chance to put my feet up before I have to get ready for what I hope is going to be yet another highlight of my trip, a tango show. I decide to sit awhile in the lobby before going to my room and sift through my photos from the day. I look up to see a glass of pisco sour being put on the low table in front of me. Initially I think the drink has been delivered to the wrong guest until the bar manager comes over. 'I am sorry about the service yesterday,' he says, 'please accept a complimentary drink, have you tried a pisco sour?' I'd attempted to order a beer the day before, but a group of recently arrived American tourists had been dominating the bar. How lovely, I think, and wonder again whether it's my age or being a guest by myself which causes another act of kindness.

La Ventana Barrio de Tango is beginning to fill up by the time my driver drops me at the entrance. I'm shown to my table and take in my surroundings. I'm sat by myself, however, a charming Brazilian couple on the next table strike up conversation. The man speaks a little English while the woman can speak some Spanish; we muddle through between us, and they are intrigued by my travelling alone. Their complimentary bottle of wine appears although mine is yet to do so, despite us being seated at the same time. I try to catch the waiter's eye without luck; he seems to be more interested in the larger groups. My cynical side is guessing he's thinking more tips are likely than with a person on their own. After me waiting several more minutes, the Brazilian couple manage to get the server's attention, and a bottle of Malbec is unceremoniously dumped on my table. I'm not usually a fuerte red wine drinker, I'd take a glass of chilled white wine any day, although I occasionally enjoy a lighter merlot or cabernet sauvignon with a meal, however this wine is delicious and seems appropriate for the occasion.

I'm still waiting for my dinner order to be taken despite tables around me having already been served. Eventually my waiter takes my order, and I don't have to wait long before my steak arrives, it's delicious; flavoursome, juicy, and well worth the delay. And the by now second glass of Malbec provides the perfect accompaniment.

There is enough time for my dessert order to be taken before the lights are dimmed and music starts up, telling us the show is beginning. A group of musicians stand onstage as the curtains are parted, the music is robust and sets the mood well for the spectacle we're about to see, immediately capturing the passion of the tango. I can conjure up images in my mind of the sultry, steamy atmosphere of the bars in La Boca. Two pairs of dancers appear from the wings and circle around before moving towards each other to adopt the signature hold of the Argentine tango. Don't get me wrong when I say the dancing's okay, because it is, but I can't help comparing it to the TV show, Strictly Come Dancing. Perhaps it has to do with my critical eye when it comes to dance but the pro dancers on that programme would win hands down. The music however is superb.

    I glance around and notice everyone has not only finished their dessert but most of the tables have been cleared of the remnants. I'm still waiting for mine. My waiter is nowhere in sight, and the one or two servers who are still around don't seem to want to know. I'm feeling distinctively peed off with the service, first the wine then having to wait for my main course order to be taken, now this. It's as if I don't exist. I stand up and make my way past other tables in an effort to find someone; I'm guessing it's break time for the waiters, eventually someone appears and goes in search of my dessert. However, when it arrives it isn't what I ordered. By this time, I've had enough of being treated what feels like a second-class citizen. Whether it's the fact I'm alone, my age or because I'm a woman, I don't know, but at no stage have I been given an apology for the bad service. I make my way upstairs to the reception area where two men look at me in surprise. I know making the complaint in Spanish would probably be more accepting, but my grasp of the language isn't good enough and I end up reverting to English. Another person appears from downstairs, I'm guessing he's the restaurant manager, he gives me some excuse about a misunderstanding with my order but no apology about the poor service. I feel at this point I'm being humoured rather than being taken seriously.

I ask someone to call for a cab to take me back to my hotel. 'Please, come back to your table, we will give you a complimentary bottle of champagne,' one of the staff says, trying to guide me downstairs. I'm too angry to accept and ask again about a cab. The noise from the street outside is raucous and I know nothing about the part of the city I'm in, consequently I'm reluctant to go in search of one myself. Eventually a cab is called, and the club does have the goodwill to pay for it, but the experience hasn't been a pleasant one. What should have been a great evening was ruined. However disappointed I am, I make myself think, c'est la vie, you win some you lose some, put it all down to experience Jan. And anyway, tomorrow there's another adventure to look forward to, I'm being taken out of the city.

Today, my trip takes me to an estancia, an Argentinian ranch. The minibus passes by a futuristic looking road bridge; the shape was specifically designed to resemble the way dancers lunge in the Argentine tango. I like the crossover between dance and architecture.

My group stops at the small town of San Antonio de Areco to visit a silversmith and learn more about the way in which the metal was used to decorate the horses of the gauchos, the ranchmen who work on the estancias. Up to forty kilos of silverware were worn by the horses on festive occasions, from bridles and stirrups to belts studded with silver decoration. I spot a brilliantly blue and yellow parrot and take a photo to send back to my grandchildren. His bulgy eyes dart about, as if keeping guard over the many valuable artefacts in the display cases.

Surprisingly, the setting when we arrive at the estancia looks like it could be out of a Constable painting There are voluminous grey and white clouds, large areas of grass and a variety of familiar shaped trees, making the setting more akin to the English countryside than the dry, dusty surroundings I was expecting. However, it's still only springtime here and the high temperatures expected each summer have yet to take effect on the colour of the terrain.

The only unfamiliar tree is an El Umbo bush, I'm told when I ask the name, with branches protruding from the trunk close to the ground. Its wide canopy provides shelter from the sun in hot weather, rather like the mesquite or the Andean paper tree I'd seen in Cusco.

We're led round to the stables where our transport awaits us, horse, or wagon. Now, I have ridden before, in fact I was lucky enough to have horse riding lessons included as an option in my sixth form at school, but to say it's been a while would be an understatement. There was one time I went horse riding in Spain, but the experience was hairy and scary when the leaders decided to whip the horses into a canter on their way back and one of my feet came loose from the stirrup. I saw the main road from Girona to Barcelona looming ahead and getting frighteningly close. I was in a panic but luckily my horse knew to take a sharp turn a mere ten meters before we reached it, and we somehow diverted onto the track back to the stables. I vowed then I would never go on a horse again. However, standing here now, I'm thinking I can't go through the reminder of my life turning down opportunities I'm not likely to experience again. And so, I put one foot in the stirrup and with help, haul my free leg over the wide girth of my equine companion.

There is no sign of cattle as we ride, but instead fields of crops, and I wonder if this isn't a working ranch as such but purely a tourist attraction. Nevertheless, the horse ride has a relaxed chill about it, although I'm still aware of having to keep my balance from aloft. The only other older person in the group comments on how well I ride. 'You look very comfortable on the horse,' he says. Little did he know I'm hanging on for grim death. The situation isn't helped by my horse trying to nibble at another one, only to get a nip back. This causes it to twitch and suddenly veer away from its companion, causing me to hang on even more tightly, and I do mean, hang on!

Beer, wine, and empanadas await us on our return from horse riding, we stand round and chat; most are Brazilians again but by speaking English and a little Spanish on my part, we manage to communicate. We're invited to go and look at the barbecue where two long racks sit over hot coals with sausages, chicken, pork, beef loin, and ribs cooking nicely. The smell is mouth-wateringly heavenly. Salads are being placed on two long tables and bottles of red and white wine begin to be opened and poured. 'Salut,' we all say and chink our glasses with our newfound friends.

We don't have to wait long until we're seated and large trays of the meats we've seen cooking, appear. The servers are wearing wide, flat berets, plain shirts and trousers tucked into their boots. I know its all very cheesy and only for us tourists but I'm enjoying the experience. They also carry a knife tucked into their belt at the back, a façon; this is a typical weapon of a gaucho who would use it to fight with as well as to eat with. Both the food and drink are plentiful, and I enjoy the chance to sit back, relax and chat while I feast on the variety of food in front of me.

When we've finished our meal, we're entertained by folk singing and dancing, including the chance to join in the fun, and followed by a demonstration of horsemanship showing the special bond between gaucho and his trusty friend.

On our way back to the city at the end of the afternoon, I get an insight into another side of Buenos Aires when we pass a number of grand houses, once the summer homes of the gentry in the pre-nineteen sixties. It certainly gives one an idea of how much wealth there was at that time. In total contrast, we pass the favela type homes which have grown up on either side of the highway. Known here as villas miserias, or slums as we might refer to them, they are a stark reminder of the difference in wealth still among the Portenas, the name given to inhabitants of Buenos Aires.

I have a free day today so take my time over breakfast. I think back to all the rushed breakfasts on this trip due to the number of early pick up times but appreciate it's all part and parcel of fitting in as much as possible. I make the most of the opportunity now and choose a selection of fruit with a glass of guava juice, then decide to follow that up with rice crispies, an odd choice to some people but I never have them at home, although it was the cereal I ate growing up. Somehow the memory of my childhood is even more heartwarming when I'm away by myself.

And then what, pancakes to follow or egg, bacon et cetera? Choices, choices! The pastries look inviting too. I decide on egg, bacon, tomato, and mushrooms but pass on the hash browns, sausages, beans. There is only so much my stomach can take. I do however wrap a muffin and banana in a napkin; they will do perfectly for later. I also have sachets of cappuccinos, brought from home, and a couple of energy bars in my case. They will both make good appetite satisfiers should the need arise.

My free day affords me the chance to walk the city, something I always enjoy but have missed doing on this trip because of the fullness of the schedule. I pick up a city map from the front desk and head off, not sure of my route but happy to let my legs see where they take me. The city is marked out in a grid system making it easy to navigate and is relatively flat, providing comfortable walking.

The art museum, Museo Nacional de Bellas Artes isn't far away; I make that my first stop and spend a pleasant hour there, browsing. This may not be a revelation to many people, but I've learnt not to try and look at too many paintings in one visit but to find a few which capture my attention and then take time to study them. More insightful and memorable to my way of thinking.

I emerge into the brilliant sunshine and see a small craft market across the way in the park area. Ooh, I do love a good market! Twenty minutes later I've bought a couple of cute tops for my granddaughters and a small selection of handmade chocolates (for me), before briefly returning to my room to deposit my purchases and to enjoy a quick cappuccino and muffin from breakfast.

This time I turn in a different direction out of the hotel and find myself in a residential area where the streets are lined with buildings, three and four storeys high in the Spanish colonial style, and in that respect not dissimilar to ones I saw in Santiago. I come across small parks and tree lined squares as I walk, with shady areas to sit and ponder, providing tranquillity in the bustling city. Children play on slides and swings in some of them, while parents or grandparents keep a watchful eye, office workers on their lunch break sit and read, making the most of their precious time before they have to return to work. I indulge in one of my favourite pastimes, people watching, and soak up the atmosphere.

I come upon a street sign in a quiet road, Calle Arturo Toscanini, named after the composer, and realise the building on my right is in fact the opera house. It's beginning to drizzle and I take shelter inside. I find out they do tours, some with an English-speaking guide, but sadly the one in an hour's time and the last of the day in English, is fully booked. What a shame, I would have loved to take a look round and compare it to the Royal Opera House in Covent Garden.

By the time I return to the hotel it's late afternoon and my body is feeling weary but content, having enjoyed my day of wandering. As I'd eaten rack of lamb last night and a huge steak at the tango club, I think tonight will be pasta or salad. I conclude, the artisan chocolate I bought today would make the perfect dessert.

My time in Buenos Aires is at an end and has been fun, apart from the tango show, and it's a city I'd like to revisit one day. I had met an English couple in the hotel who were here for one reason only; the wife was mad about the Argentine tango, and the two of them either had a lesson each day or visited one of the many bars where people would just get up and dance it. I wouldn't mind coming here again and learning how to dance like that. But for now, I'm leaving Argentina with many wonderful memories, and moving on to my fifth country; my onward journey is by ferry across the widest river in the world to my next port of call, Uruguay.

Approaching Perito Merino Glacier

Overlooking glacier, the shades of blue are unbelievable.

Colourful loos in the La Boca area of Buenos Aires

Leisurely horse ride on the estancia

Uruguay

My decision to pay a short visit to Uruguay was solely to add another country to my list while I was visiting South America. I know little about it except for the name of the capital, that it is a big beef producing country, and has a national football team. I also know it has a city called Fray Bentos, the same name as a well known tinned corned beef product. That appeals to my sense of humour.

So far on my trip. I've visited the highest administrative capital in the world, La Paz, sailed on the highest lake, Titicaca, stayed in the Atacama Desert, considered to be the driest place on the globe, crossed the widest road, Ninth Avenue in Buenos Aires, and today I'm taking the ferry on the widest river in the world, Rio de la Plata, one hundred and forty miles at its widest.

The journey by ferry from Buenos Aires is one often taken by tourists on a day trip who, probably just like me, want to visit another country. My guide checks me in at the terminal and my luggage is whisked away to be put onboard. So nice not to have to carry it on and off the boat. She indicates to an escalator for me to take. 'The embarkation lounge is up there,' she tells me, pointing to the floor above. I follow her instructions and find two lounges, one already crowded with passengers waiting to board, another quieter one with next to nobody in. I'm guessing they are either for different classes or possibly Uruguayan or foreign nationals. I look at my boarding pass but don't find anything on it to help me and I can't see any official around. Oh well, what's the worse that can happen to me, I ask myself, I could get chucked out, I suppose, but so what? Certainly, as I've gotten older, I've become less worried about what people might think. I choose the quieter lounge, no-one approaches me, and I sit in ignorant bliss until boarding starts.

My ticket is checked onboard and a crew member points to up the stairs where another one is there to greet me, holding a tray of sparkling wine. Maybe I was in the correct waiting lounge after all! Before long we set sail on the hour and a half journey; Wi-Fi connection is good, allowing me to upload my photos and chats to WhatsApp about my final day in Buenos Aires.

I see a welcome sign Bienvenidos a Uruguay when I disembark and collect my suitcase from the conveyor belt. Immigration is straightforward and there is a driver waiting for me outside the terminal building, holding a card with my name on.

After a short journey, we stop outside a small characterful looking hotel in a quiet cobblestoned street. We've arrived in Colonia del Sacramento, once a Portuguese settlement and now a UNESCO world heritage site. I complete the by now familiar formalities of filling in a form in reception and showing my passport before I'm taken to my room.

'You have a room upgrade for your stay, I hope you like it,' I'm told. What is it about this trip, another upgrade? I have no idea why; I can only ponder. Maybe it's just luck. Whatever the reason, I'm happy when I look round. Whilst not the biggest one I've ever stayed in, although this was pretty spacious, the room is without doubt the most tasteful. The pitched ceiling is supported at two ends by large stone walls, rather like the kind you see lining narrow Devon lanes, on one long side two windows are framed by dark wooden shutters while on the last wall there are paintings of the local area. The bathroom has a walk-in shower and on the shelf are a selection of lightly fragranced toiletries in eucalyptus and lavender. The towels, all carefully folded and arranged, have pretty embroidered motifs of lavender as well.

Returning to the main area, my bed dominates one end with a chest of drawers, again in a dark wood, while at the other end is a two-seater retro sofa and coffee table. On it are sophisticated looking photography books of the area and a retro radio, although this one also has a docking station and USB port. The coffee is real coffee, none of your sachets here, and the tea choices are wide. I make myself a hot drink and pore through the books; the place has the feel of a luxury country cottage and part of me would like to sit back and enjoy, however the photos have whetted my appetite and I'm keen to explore. A quick unpack (I'm only here for one night) and I'm off out.

My hotel is in the Barro Historico (historic quarter); remnants of the old city wall still exist, built with stone similar to the type in my hotel room, and there is a drawbridge which is still functioning. Old stone buildings, with yellow and lime green lichen growing in the walls' crevices, line the narrow cobblestone streets. These have blue and white ceramic road signs which add to the character. There are some newer houses too, but most are single storey and simply designed with two windows at the front and a door in the middle, helping them to blend in with the original buildings.

I catch odd glimpses of wisteria beginning to show signs of flowering as I walk and come across the ruins of what was once a cathedral. There is a tall lighthouse directly behind them, so close it appears to be part of the structure, although its whiteness starkly contrasts with the dark stone remains of the religious edifice.

I stroll on and see a row of golf buggies lining a wider road, obviously a useful way to explore the old part of the town, but I'm not tempted to add to my list of modes of transport, never having driven one before. And anyway, I'm in relax mode by now. A bar in the square looks inviting; the last ferry back to Buenos Aires has left and the place is deserted. I sit and enjoy my beer before returning to my hotel, clicking away with my camera at the many pretty sights on offer, as I go.

Chivito is on the menu, the Uruguayan national dish, in the hotel restaurant when I sit down for dinner, but my choice is fish and pumpkin risotto with a complimentary glass of bubbly to accompany it. Not usually a risotto person, I'm glad I made it my choice, it's creamy, light, and flavoursome. My enjoyment doesn't end with the main course either, the piece de resistance proves to be the dessert. I've never had cheese and ice cream together before, this is a revelation; brie wrapped in a feather light filo pastry parcel served piping hot with guava ice cream. The whole meal has been super tasty and well worth the price. I'm even more pleased when eighteen per cent is taken off the bill. Evidently, if you pay by credit card, this discount is applied because the government is trying to attract tourism. An added bonus to a perfect meal.

It's a relatively leisurely start the next morning compared to the many early ones on the trip. I take my time to say goodbye to my room, a few days holed up here wouldn't have been a hardship, before my driver collects me at nine o'clock for the two-hour drive to Montevideo.

The roads are relatively traffic free and I opt to sit back and listen to two episodes of Desert Island Discs. I'm not generally a radio listener at home, but a few years earlier I had been chatting to someone on a flight who said she downloaded Desert Island Discs programmes for when she was away, and it gave me the same idea. They're a good way of passing the time on long journeys and make a pleasant accompaniment when you're travelling solo. The length of each programme isn't too long for my attention span but enough to allow me to learn something about the person. Today my choice is Marcus Waring, the chef, and Zaha Hadid, architect of the aquatic centre for the 2012 London Olympics; quite different personalities but both make entertaining listening.

It's too early to check in when we arrive at the hotel and I don't have anything booked until my city tour in the afternoon, so I take a leisurely walk along the Rambla Gandhi, the thirteen-mile promenade which hugs the Atlantic coastline and the shores of the River Plate. There is a gentle breeze, and the easy flat walking makes a pleasant change from the hours I've spent being driven. I pass a rugby pitch between the walkway and the sea, and recall that, like Argentina, the country has a national team which regularly plays against England. The pitch is unoccupied, similarly there is no-one in the sea or on the beach; I guess it's early in the season still and it will be sometime before the water temperature warms up.

The minibus, with mostly Brazilians again as my fellow tourists, takes us to see the main sights on the city tour; I don't know whether it's because Montevideo is similar to other Spanish influenced places I've seen on this trip, or whether it's because of the length of time I've been away, but my interest threshold has been reached. Whatever the reason, I don't take in as much as I probably should. Congress Palace, sporting banners advertising the various political parties who will take part in the political election in a few days time,

Independence Square with its statute of Artigas, the soldier who played an important role in the history of Uruguay, and the art deco looking Palacio Salvo, come and go. The other passengers, who are all considerably younger, treat me with deference and I'm offered assistance to get in and out of the minibus every time we make a stop. Part of me wants to show my independence but another part thinks, how nice it is to be treated with respect. And my knees are glad of the help after nearly six weeks of in and out, off and on various modes of transport.

Our final stop of the tour is the Mercado Agricola (farmer's market) with a pretty decorative ceramic archway above the entrance. There is a mixture of stalls, shops and stand-up eateries, and I'm tempted to buy a chivito. Literally translated as little goat, it contains steak, ham, cheese, fried egg, tomatoes, olives, mayonnaise, and lettuce in a bread roll. We're only given thirty minutes to stop here so I decide against it and resolve to have one for my dinner; there will be plenty of time to enjoy a chivito later this evening. Instead, I take the time to browse around at the array of foodstuffs for sale. The market is not dissimilar to London's Borough Market with a variety of produce on sale, both fresh foods and packaged items.

Back at my hotel later, I pack up the few bits and pieces I've used and then take one last stroll along the Rambla before heading to the food court in the shopping mall nearby. There is another gorgeous sunset with thin elongated lines of dark grey clouds over a pretty pink and blue sky, and the pale sun slipping into the sea.

With a beer in hand and a ridiculously large chivito and fries to finish off the day, I am content; the visit to the fifth country on my itinerary has been brief but well worth it.

My whole trip to South America is nearly at an end, tomorrow I have a flight back to Buenos Aires, followed by an onward flight to my last stop and the final country of my six-week trip. Vamos Brasil!

Chivito - Uruguay's national dish

Brazil

My cab takes me over the border, from here I have a short drive to the national park and to the hotel I'd fallen in love with thirteen years earlier, the Cataratas. It looks as beautiful as I remember; pinkwashed walls, manicured lawns and swaying palm trees, the only hotel in the national park and sitting directly opposite one of the new natural wonders of the world, Iguacu Falls. A series of two hundred and seventy-five vertical drops, they create the largest waterfall system on the planet and form a natural border between Argentina, Brazil, and Paraguay. Depending on which country you're in, the spelling varies, Iguacu, Iguassu, or Iguazu.

Other people I've met while I've been away have raved about Easter Island or Machu Picchu, and how those places hold special meaning to them, but for me it's the falls; my spiritual home, a special place where I feel more at one with myself than anywhere else in the world. And that is the reason I want to finish my trip here.

The layout of the hotel is hacienda style; only two floors high, it has a wide veranda across the complete width at the back allowing guests to look out onto the lush gardens. Colourful flowers are dotted about, and varieties of orchids nestle in the trunks of trees. I can see the blue of the swimming pool peeping through the shrubbery and the sunlight shimmering on the surface, inviting me in. The temptation is strong but once I've unpacked, my watch is telling me I have something more important to do.

I come back down to the lobby just in time to see the last bus leaving the park, taking with it the final group of visitors.

For the rest of the daylight, guests at the hotel have the falls to themselves and I intend making the most of it. I cross the narrow road outside the hotel and settle down on the steps to watch the swallows dive in and out of the curtains of water. The sun begins to sink in the sky; the water takes on a golden glow before the light gradually weakens and starts to disappear. I sit with the few other hotel guests and maintain a respectful silence, collectively sharing the special moment, a sense of calm gradually taking me over.

I rise early the next day and walk down to the promontory sitting over the water, the walkway which, within a short while of the park opening, will be packed with visitors. At this time of the morning, I have the falls to myself, as I'd hoped, my only company being the sound of the water rippling and trickling its way over the moss-covered rocks beneath me. Here the gentle flow is in stark contrast to the gushing, tumbling walls of water forming an arc on three sides about a hundred metres away. I rest my elbows on the rail and look up at the wondrous sight of the Garganta del Diablo (Devil's Gorge) on the Argentinian side, majestic in the distance. On my last visit I'd taken a helicopter ride over it and seen from above its size and grandeur. The water's sheer power fills me with energy.

I enjoy fifteen minutes of seclusion before I hear other hotel guests who, like me, are making the most of the opportunity to see the falls before the buses arrive. Breakfast calls and I make my way back to the hotel and go straight into the restaurant. A buffet awaits me, spread across three long tables in addition to the cooking station. The choice is mouth watering. I'm not the most adventurous person when it comes to food, particularly at breakfast, but after I've had my go to juice and plate of fresh fruit, I spy a fourth table laden with bottles of champagne and the wherewithal for making a Bloody Mary. I have nothing planned until the afternoon, my time is my own till then, perhaps I should be adventurous. Although all the ingredients are there; vodka, tomato juice, Worcestershire sauce, salt, pepper, slices of lemon and ice, I've no idea of the proportions for Bloody Mary, so ask one of the servers to sort me out. My drink comes with a decorative toucan headed stirrer and looking very pretty. I feel a bit of a fraud having a cocktail at this time of the day, but hey ho, I'm on holiday, so why not. Whilst I can taste the pepperiness and generous measure of vodka, I can't get over the fact that I don't like and never have liked tomato juice. Why I think this time might be different I don't know, but in the end, I put my cocktail to one side and fetch a glass of champers to accompany my eggs, bacon, and hash browns instead.

The rest of my morning is spent by the pool; the sun is hot and the humidity high, but I cool off in the water then sit under the wide parasol and read on my Kindle. One of the pool attendants comes round and offers me a complimentary fruit skewer, leftovers from breakfast I'm guessing, which I accept. Later the same attendant appears again, this time with ice towels, which he picks up out of a freezer box with tongs. I'm reminded of a rude joke and give out an involuntary laugh. He gives me an enquiring look, but I don't explain. The meaning would definitely get lost in translation.

I retire to my room and eat my 'lunch', a pastry from breakfast and a banana, washed down by a cup of tea, and prepare myself for the afternoon's excursion, something I'd booked with the hotel concierge the night before, a boat ride to see the falls close up, or so I thought.

I catch the bus taking visitors between the falls and the entrance gates into the national park but alight a stop earlier than the other travellers. I don't have to wait long till my mode of transport appears to take me through the forest to the boat jetty. The other people onboard, children and adults, jabber away in Portuguese, excited by what's in store. The temperature has risen and is now thirty-eight degrees, feeling even hotter because of the humidity, and I think how lovely it's going to be when we get in the boat and have the spray of the water cooling us down. Little did I know….!

We arrive at the landing stage, and I'm asked, 'Wet or dry?'

A couple in the group call out enthusiastically, 'Wet.' The people around me all nod their heads in agreement and look at me approvingly when I shrug my shoulders and agree. We're given rainproof hooded ponchos to put on and transferred to a boat. I notice there's no-one taking the dry option so am reassured I've chosen the better option.

The boat soon picks up speed as we near the main body of water; it suddenly bounces as we hit the wake of another boat and we begin to feel the torrent of the water crashing into the river, making the ride very bumpy. The boat changes course and heads towards one of the waterfalls, I realise what was meant by the wet option now. Instead of what I thought was going to be a pleasant excursion to see the falls close up, now turns into an amusement park ride as the water comes gushing over, completely swamping us from above. My companions whoop and scream as the boat ducks in and out of the waterfalls, each one drenching us. I'd had the sense to leave my camera behind but had forgotten about my watch, my precious Rotary, the one usually worn on my travels. I wrap it under my T shirt, praying the water won't penetrate.

The boat continues to rush and weave; I thought getting nearer would mean having a better view but in reality, we're crashing in and out of the falls so much, I can't see a thing. The enthusiasm, however, is infectious and I find myself joining in with the 'Whoos' and 'Aaghs'. The excursion hasn't been what I was expecting but it certainly is an experience. And I'm pleased to say my Rotary watch has survived.

The next day I have a car collecting me to take the trip across the border to the Argentinian side of the falls. The drive takes about an hour and a half and I collect another stamp in my passport on the way. When we arrive, I follow the crowds to the small train which will drop us off nearer to the falls. People point to a few monkeys in the trees on the way and the coati sniffing around on the ground. It's slightly cooler than yesterday, a mere thirty-four degrees, but again the humidity makes it feel hotter. Thunderstorms are forecast for tomorrow; however, I'll be heading home then.

The Argentinian side has three distinct trails to follow. My first stop is the Garganta del Diablo; I remember the last time I was here there was an abundance of brilliant blue butterflies, however this time I see none. My guide tells me it's because the winter was colder this year. The viewpoint for this most spectacular of waterfalls is crazily crowded and I have to wait patiently before I can squeeze myself through to get a good look. There are clear reflections of the blue sky in the river before the falls, here it's like a millpond, then slowly but surely the water gathers momentum as it gets nearer and nearer to the precipice, before roaring over the edge and crashing down into the abyss. I can appreciate the force which must be generated by hydro electric power as I watch.

In the distance to my left, I can make out the Brazilian side and the promontory where I'd stood the previous day. Now it's crowded with people jostling, as we are, to get the perfect photo opportunity.

Another trail where the falls are quieter and the path is more shaded, provide welcome shelter from the sun, now high in the sky. The setting is different from the Brazilian side, here the experience is more immersive, passing close by smaller waterfalls and rivulets. I decide to forego another trail, (I'd done all three on my previous visit) and instead, take the train back to the entrance. I'm hungry, despite another big breakfast, maybe it's the fresh air, and decide to try a tasty steak in the restaurant. It certainly lives up to Argentina's reputation as a great beef producing country; the whole meal is delicious.

By the time we've driven back to the Brazilian side and reached the hotel, it is late afternoon. I sit and drink a beer to quench my thirst and people watch by the pool before returning to my room to start packing for the final time.

The next day I take the first bus of the morning from outside my hotel; it's still too early for the tourists to enter the park, this one is for people who work in the gift shops and eateries further down the road. I alight and take the lift down to beside the falls, to see them from a different angle this time. There is a huge expanse of falling water on my left, so close I can feel its spray. The view is spectacular, and I thank my lucky stars I've been able to experience it not once but twice. There is just enough time for one last look before catching the bus back to my hotel to get ready for my departure.

Waiting for the car to take me to the airport for my last two flights of the trip, I think back to all that's happened before I leave beautiful Iguacu and head home to the UK. It seems appropriate somehow when the heavens open and the forecasted thunderstorm starts, as if the skies above are heralding the end of my stay in South America. Six countries in six weeks, thirteen very different modes of transport including eleven flights, a horse and one slide, and goodness knows how many flights of steps I've climbed or kilometres I've walked. I've met many friendly travellers, too many to count, but particularly Australians, collected fourteen more stamps in my passport and, most importantly, am still alive to tell the tale. Someone asked me before I started the trip if I had any doubts about travelling around as a single woman, but no, I didn't. And my guides and drivers (mostly men), without exception, proved to be professional in every way.

Independent travel can work for the older person; you don't have to be brave or gung ho. With good organisation and a willingness to give it a try, you can still see the world if you want to. Sometimes it's better to think of the can dos than the cannots. If you think you can, then you can. It doesn't mean everything is possible, I'm not naïve enough to think that. But so often as we get older, we talk ourselves out of things or allow ourselves to be influenced by what others think regarding the capabilities of older people. The seeds of doubt creep into our minds and suddenly our world has shrunk, metaphorically and in reality.

And when I did return from my trip unscathed, richer in culture and wiser, what did I think about my first long trip as a solo traveller, would I do it again? You betcha!

The trip in 2019 was a seventieth birthday present to myself.

My spiritual home Iguacu Falls Brazilian side

Iguacu Falls Brazilian side

CENTRAL AMERICA

Costa Rica

My itinerary for the five-week trip will take in five countries and travel the length and breadth of Central America, the part of the globe between the United States and South America. I'll be staying on the Pacific Ocean, the Atlantic and, a first for me, the Caribbean, as well as inland.

My plane lands in San Jose and, as with all the stops, a car has been arranged to collect me. The most noticeable feature about my hotel is the artwork, it's everywhere, in the lobby, the bar, the corridors, the rooms, and even the pool area. They're not of a specific genre, the collection includes portraits, scenes, 3D works, all hung alongside each other, but generally they are contemporary pieces and certainly bring added character to the place.

There is a sign on the same floor as my room saying piscina, swimming would be an ideal way to uncoil the wrinkles after an eleven-hour flight. Unpacking is done quickly, (I'm only here for two nights), and then I head to the pool; a pleasant way to start to my trip.

My alarm has had to be set for six am the next day, breakfast hasn't begun yet when I come downstairs, but a tray of muffins has been left out for the early risers to help themselves to, along with tea and coffee. The first visit is to a coffee plantation and by the time we arrive there the temperature has already shot up, despite the early hour. I'm in a group of a dozen or so from different countries; some English, a Dutch couple and a French family. The guide points out a toucan to us in a nearby tree while we're waiting for our tour to start, it's long beak and colourful plumage making it easy to spot. I had seen one at the Iguacu Falls, high up in a tree, but this one is nearer, enabling me to get a closer look. Do you remember the bird used to feature in Guinness adverts? Now, I wonder how that came about, after all, the connection between a bird and a stout isn't immediately obvious, at least not to me.

Although I'm not much of a coffee drinker, usually restricting my input to one a day, and that in the form of a cappuccino, I love the smell, and the aroma as we're shown around is intoxicating. Evidently Costa Rican coffee is a valuable commodity, the beans fetching many thousands of dollars at auction. The fact that all coffee flowers in this country are hand picked probably contributes to their cost, as well as the taste of course. Although it's only the first day of my trip, I dismiss the fact that I'll have to carry any purchases around for the next five weeks and buy two bags of Costa Rican coffee beans for my kids. Seems silly to be here and not take some home with me.

Next, it's on to the Poas volcano; there are five around the valley in which San Jose sits, this one rising to two thousand seven hundred metres above sea level. A marked increase in the emission of gases over the last half century, has caused acid rain damage to the surrounding agricultural plantations.

I'm fascinated by volcanoes, have even choreographed a dance using them as a stimulus; it started with the dancers in a circle performing a Graham fall forward in canon then overbalancing and tumbling into the abyss. So many actions come to mind; bubbling, sparking, exploding, coursing, sliding, sticking, to name but a few. Rudolf Laban would be proud of me!

We've been told we'll only be able to visit the volcano for twenty minutes and I want to make the most of the first time

I've ever seen one. I keep up with the guide at the front, walking briskly along the inclined path till we come to a viewing stand looking down on the crater. The crowd ooh and ah, and point out to each other any slight sign of activity, we watch the odd bubble, looking a bit like soup when it's being heated up, and then a puff of smoke, or maybe it's water vapour? The volcano is emitting large amounts of gas and vapour from the different fumaroles located in the inner cone of the crater, but we can still watch the activity through them.

All too soon our allocated time is up, and we have to leave. The visit has given me a fascinating insight into the workings of a volcano; what a great first day it's been.

The next day, I leave San Jose to visit Tortuguero National Park. The minibus arrives early to collect me, then I'm taken to a meeting point to catch a coach. We make a few stops to pick up other people on the way, however, at one hotel there is a delay when the couple being collected aren't in their lobby. Everyone glares at them when they eventually get on the bus until the guide explains it was their tour company who gave them the wrong time. I make sure I give them a warm smile at the next stop but secretly I'm thinking what I would have done for an extra thirty minutes in bed. The journey is long and arduous, the roads, once we get off the highway, are of a poor quality and the driver has to go slowly, often having to manage his way around potholes. There are a limited number of flights to Tortuguero but they're expensive.

At one place, the coach has to come to a stop; the road we're on goes through a banana plantation and in front of us is a line of banana mules, a hanging conveyor belt on which huge sticks of the fruit, covered in blue plastic, are being transported directly from the trees to the production line inside. In a building to our left, we can see dozens of people working to sift, sort and package them before being sent off for sale.

Our journey takes six hours in total, by coach then boat, and by the time we reach our lodge I'm regretting my decision not to have opted for the private tour of Costa Rica my travel company had first quoted. The alternative I chose was to join a group tour at a saving of fifteen hundred pounds for the ten days. I'd taken group excursions at various times on my trip to South America, and it seemed like a good way to cut back on the budget, (Costa Rica in particular is expensive evidently). I realise now that was a mistake on my part, everything has taken so much longer in a group.

The chalets are dotted throughout the grounds of the lodge, rather like a Hansel and Gretel setting, and look rather cute with wooden steps leading up to the door and a rocking chair on the small patio to greet me. The room appears to be comfy enough and has windows taking up two sides, giving a real sense of being in and among the jungle, and I can hear birds chattering and movement in the trees outside, suggesting creatures are nearby. The only problem with the room is that there are no blinds and the curtains don't quite do their job, making it impossible to enjoy any privacy. I decide the shower will have to function as a dressing room as well, either that or getting dressed and undressed in the dark.

We have a guided walk on the itinerary this afternoon; it's hot and humid by now, although the trees do offer a fair amount of shade. I don't know whether it's the heat or tiredness, or the fact that I don't find our guide very committed, but I'm not fully engaged and when he disappears to take a phone call in the middle of his talk, I decide to leave the group and find a bench beside the riverfront from where I can watch the boats going to and fro on the water; a more pleasant and interesting activity.

We have another early start the next day, five thirty to be precise. I shower and manoeuvre myself in the small bathroom space to get dressed then wait with my fellow passengers for the boat to takes us on our river safari. Will I ever catch up on my sleep I wonder?

Our boat driver points out an American alligator (they only grow to a maximum of two metres so not too scary), porcupine, an iguana, a lizard, and many distinct species of birds. I soon realise my camera isn't powerful enough to do any of them justice, instead of taking photos I sit back and admire the environs which surround me.

Back on dry land, I sit in the rocking chair outside my door and look around. It has rained overnight, and the greenness of the surrounding trees and plants is even more vibrant now. I can hear something rustling in the tree above and not far in front of me and see branches moving, too much for it to be a bird or a small creature. Something black and orangy brown appears and disappears among the foliage, swinging from tree to tree; it's a monkey, too big to be a capuchin but likely to be a howler monkey. I'd heard them early that morning, after the rain stopped hammering on the roof, their barks and roars marking out their territory. Evidently, they're one of the loudest land animals to exist. The creature appears again then I lose sight of it, no doubt moving on just as swiftly as it had arrived, seeking adventure elsewhere.

In the afternoon there is a boat trip to Tortuguero beach, and the rain has returned, not as much as during the night but showery, squally weather with low, dull grey clouds in the sky. We visit the long beach where every year turtles come ashore to lay their eggs then bury them in the sand until they're ready to hatch. As I look out at the wide expanse of ocean, I get a sense of how hazardous the hatchlings' journey must be. Only one in a thousand hatched eggs survive, either because of the birds or the ferocious Atlantic.

Other than the beach there is little to see in Tortuguero; a row of souvenir shops, a few eateries catering for the tourist market, a conservation place, which is closed, and that's it. However, I'm brightened by the colourfully painted basura (recycling bin), and a decorative sign created with buttons.

I decide to celebrate my last evening here with a cocktail, a Mai Thai. Just as I had set myself a challenge on my South America trip of how many different modes of transport I could use, this time it's cocktails. I sit and sip, enjoying the dark and white rum combined with the fruity taste, and peruse my stay here. Interesting, would be an apt description, but nothing more. Other people I'd spoken to at home prior to my trip had raved about their visit here; whether it was the fact that I'd done something similar in Borneo and therefore the experience wasn't new, or whether it was the journey, or perhaps the poor guide, I don't know. However, a new adventure lies ahead for me tomorrow, onward, and upward, a different area of Costa Rica awaits.

The eight hours in transit to La Fortuna was long but worth it; my room is bigger than the whole of my downstairs space at home and I have the most glorious view of the Arenal volcano. Its perfect conical shape reminds me of the image you see at the start of Paramount film productions. Outside the patio doors, my private sitting area is surrounded by cacti, birds of paradise and ginger flowers, among many others. The sun is casting a shadow over one side of the volcano while the other is bathed in bright sunlight, the birds are singing away and I think this must be what paradise is like.

After a week or so of early starts, I don't have to get up at the crack of dawn the next day and for that I'm thankful. As I've alluded to in other chapters, there is always a balance to find between wanting to fit in as much as possible, of seeing places before the tourist crowds arrive, and slowing down the pace enough to truly enjoy the experience.

The breakfasts here are fabulous with so much variety on offer, it's difficult to choose. I have my usual fresh fruit to start and then opt for a compote of Greek yogurt, tamarind jam, granola, and strawberries, all washed down with an energy drink of beetroot, ginger, orange, and guava juice. I would like to pretend how healthily I'm eating but the pancakes look tempting, and of course, they have to be with maple syrup.

Today involves another river trip and I'm hoping it offers something better or at least different from Tortuguero. This one is on the River Frio at the Cano Negro Wildlife Refuge.

The guide is excellent and I'm coming to realise how integral these people are to the whole experience. There are monkeys galore to see; howlers again but white-faced capuchins as well, who we spend some time watching as they leap precariously from one tree to another, as if they're trying to outdo one another. Iguanas come into vision, languidly lying along branches, basking in the midday sun, and lizards too. Our boat captain draws the guide's attention to something on our right hand side and points in that direction; initially I see nothing unusual but then my eyes open wide when I, along with my fellow passengers, spy a crocodile on the bank, its colouring and the shading of its scales, ingeniously providing camouflage. The only thing about it which moves is the occasional opening of its eyelids to reveal bulgy, stary eyes, but for most of the time it remains absolutely still. Fascinating!

By the time we return to the riverbank and get off the boat, I am buzzing from the experience. Lunch is included too; it says chicken sandwich but looks like a baguette when it arrives and served with cassava chips. Very tasty. A great morning and an infinitely better experience than Tortuguero.

The spa pool bar is heaving when I return to the hotel, but the main pool is uncrowded; I have a refreshing swim then sit in the shade under one of the umbrellas. It's twenty-seven degrees by now but without the humidity I'd experienced in Tortuguero; I read and sift through my photos and generally make the most of my downtime. I like it here.

Housekeeping has left a plate of treats in my room for me; a mix of marzipan and chocolate sweets, along with a handwritten note welcoming me to the hotel. I love these extra little touches. I decide my breakfast, lunch and now this will be enough for me to eat today; instead of dinner I take a long shower and pamper myself with the various body creams left out for me, and then, by nine, I'm in bed, because, surprise, surprise, there is another early start in the morning, this time searching for sloths.

I wish I could say the sloth tour is exciting but in reality, it's pretty underwhelming. We do see six of them in total, brown throated three toed ones evidently, but they just look like big blobs high up in the tree. It's only through the guide's binoculars and the telescopic lens of his camera that one can make out their features. But then, if you're an animal which moves less than forty metres in a day, it makes sense the sightings aren't likely to be extraordinary.

At the end of the walk, we stop in the forest to have a traditional Costa Rican breakfast, rice, beans, egg, cheese, and plantain. Palatable enough but, as breakfast at the hotel isn't over by the time I get back, I have a second one, including a cup of good old Rosie Lee.

On returning to my room, I take a nap to compensate for the early start that morning, and prepare myself for another adventure, because later I'm going to do something which has been on my bucket list for a long time; this afternoon I'm going zip wiring.

My minibus comes to collect me from the hotel, and we have a short fifteen-minute drive to reach the activity centre. I'm a tad nervous, not frightened, but definitely is this a wise decision moment? I'm aware I still have nearly four weeks of my trip to go; the last thing I would want is to have something happen which might put a downer on that. However, the person gearing me up doesn't give me a look as if to say, 'Are you sure you should be doing this at your age?' Which reassures me. I'm a firm believer that one should keep trying new things as one gets older, however, it's easy sometimes to let people's opinions affect your judgements. My advice would be, be aware of what other people think but don't let their views define you.

When the group is all gathered, we're given instructions and taken to a familiarisation try out, a short, one metre off the ground zip line, and then, before I've had time to draw breath, we pile into the back of an open truck and drive along the bumpy tracks, taking us higher into the hillside. The other group members are all young enough to be my grandchildren but there is a sort of camaraderie among us; some sit quietly whilst others chatter away, obviously excited about what lies ahead.

We're high up by now and I have a quick, what if my hoist breaks moment as I look down into the trees below. Will they break my fall, I ponder? I bring myself back to reality and say to myself, don't be daft, nothing is going to happen to you, and if it does, well, you've had a good life!

I hear our leader say, 'Who wants to go first?' My hand immediately shoots up.

'I'll go first,' I can hear my voice saying. You might think this odd when I don't feel that confident, but I've always thought, if you go first, you can then relax, whereas if you wait until near the end, nervousness can get the better of you.

I'm hooked on, given last minute instructions, and off I go, sailing above the canopy of tress and having the adventure of my life. I don't quite get the arrival right at the platform and slow down far too soon but better that than taking out one of the guides with a kamikaze type landing. I watch as the other eleven in the group have their turn, and I'm feeling pretty chipper when some of them give me the thumbs up and admiring nods of approval. A couple even congratulate me. 'Brava,' they say. I'm feeling as tall as the highest tree around us. I do love a bit of street cred.

The remaining ten lines pass by in a flash, and by the end of it I'm buzzing. I'd like to do it all over again, but it's time to get back into our respective minibuses and return to our hotels. Maybe another time, another place, another country.

It's probably something to do with the rush of adrenalin from the afternoon, but I'm hungry this evening. The dinner choice in the restaurant is as eclectic as breakfast, and I notice something I've never come across before. I've seen eggs cooked to order, and stir fries, also pancakes, but never a pasta station. In front of the chef is spaghetti, penne, tagliatelle, fusilli and a few more whose names I don't know, plus an array of accompaniments. I go for the spaghetti with onions, garlic, red peppers, mushrooms, cheese, and a white sauce. To have fresh pasta is a treat but to have it cooked to order in front of you is something else, and it tastes as good as I'd hoped.

I could have stayed in La Fortuna longer than the two days I've been here; I never did discover the thermal waters for which the town is known, however other places still await.

This time it's a three-hour drive to visit Monteverde and the Cloud Forest. The geographical phenomenon is formed when two contrasting climates clash: the hot and dry Pacific, and hot and wet Atlantic, creating a biodiverse environment. A series of six hanging bridges allow you to be among the trees or above their canopy. I'll pay a visit to it tomorrow but this evening I enjoy a pleasant nature walk in the grounds of my new hotel then have a relaxing jacuzzi before dinner.

The hotel restaurant is my sort of eatery; jazz playing in the background, ambient lighting, and attendant staff. I take a sip of my Screwdriver, and the waiter asks me if it's okay, when I give him the not too sure face, he pops another shot of vodka in. Definitely my sort of place.

The early morning visit, yes again, to the Cloud Forest means my guide and I have the route to ourselves. The bridges vary in length, the longest being two hundred and thirty-six metres, and each one is named after a tree growing nearby. The ice cream bean tree bridge is an unusual one. Rather like zip wiring, you hang on for dear life crossing the first one, as there is quite a bit of movement in the structure, but, before long, you go with the flow and embrace the motion. Eighty percent of the year, it rains here but I'm lucky to see it in brilliant sunshine today with an excellent guide.

My youngest granddaughter has asked me to look out for the quetzal bird; she's been learning about the Cloud Forest in a TV programme, would you believe. Amazing what kids learn about these days. We see many birds, as well as a squirrel and a tarantula but sadly no quetzal.

The early start meant I'd missed breakfast at the hotel, instead I have to 'endure' a Nutella croissant and cappuccino in the cafe after my guided walk. The server twists my arm to have some Baileys syrup in my coffee, what a hardship. From where I'm sitting, I can see the zip wiring starting up as I eat. It's tempting to give it another go but in the end I'm happy to sit and watch while I drool over my Nutella croissant.

That evening, I sit by the firepit at my hotel and chat to some of the other guests. It's been a short but pleasant outing to visit another part of Costa Rica, and to cap it all, I've learnt about the quetzal bird from my five-year-old granddaughter.

Tamarindo on the Pacific coast this time, is the next place on my itinerary; it's going to provide me with a couple of days relaxation, no early starts, no tours, nothing except what I want to do with my day. My body is ready for it; there have been some opportunities for chill time, but a great deal has been packed into my visit to Costa Rica, only nine days in all, but it feels much longer with everything I've seen and done.

That evening, I join the dozens of people and go across from my hotel to watch the sunset. There are locals, I'm guessing a regular occurrence for them, sitting on the sand or in chairs angled facing out to sea, waiting for the spectacle to begin, and horses being led back to their stables further up the beach, with the last of their customers for the day sitting astride them. A group of people are playing a game with a round trampette placed in the middle of them, one I've never seen before. I discover it's called spike ball with two players on each side, where the ball is bounced on the trampette in such a way as to make it difficult for the opposition to return.

It looks great fun. The sunset is beautiful with the silhouettes of boats against a backdrop of golden sky and orange sun.

I decide to add to my cocktail list and choose an aptly named Tamarind Sunset, tamarind liqueur, rum, mango juice, lime juice, and grenadine. It's as good as it sounds.

The next morning, I spend a leisurely hour and a half amble around the bay, people watching, waves admiring and listening to my Tina Turner and Cher playlist. The bay is full of activity; gentle surfing, the odd paraglider, dog walking, pétanque playing, there are even massages on offer. The temperature is thirty degrees Celsius but, with a pleasant breeze, the air is comfortable. Last night I'd looked up what would be the next land sighting across the Pacific Ocean, it's the island nation of Papua New Guinea. Strange how small and insignificant it makes you feel when you look out at an expanse of sea.

I spend the afternoon relaxing by the pool having found out I'm being collected at three thirty in the morning the next day. It seems I'll have a five-and-a-half-hour drive north in order to get on a plane going south. I'm not happy with the local Costa Rican company who organised this part of my trip, but I accept it's partly my fault, having opted out of a private tour. It's proven not to be such a good decision. I realise now the shared transfers in particular and the time they take, have made travelling noticeably more arduous.

So, on my last evening in Costa Rica, how would I sum up my eleven days? I've looked down into an active volcano, zip wired, seen an array of creatures for the first time, drank a fair number of cocktails, and stayed in some delightful hotels, but the travelling has been a killer. Road conditions make driving slow and I've spent much of my time sitting in a minibus being driven from one place to the next, some of which was due to poor planning. Would I want to come here again (always a good benchmark for me), no probably not, but hey, it's all an experience. Panama here I come.

View from my bedroom of the Arenal volcano

Croc at the Cano Negro Wildlife Refuge Centre

Tamarindo Bay at sunset

Monteverde Cloud Forest

Panama

The main purpose of this part of my tour around Central America is to visit the Panama Canal. Ever the romantic, I can recall learning how ships would have to sail around the continent of South America before it was built, and cross from the Atlantic to the Pacific or vice versa via Cape Horn, a longer and more treacherous route. The conquistadors as long ago as the sixteenth century had been looking for a quicker route to transport the booty they'd plundered, but it wasn't until the early twentieth century the canal was built. Carved out of dense jungle, the fifty-mile-long man-made waterway carries up to thirty-eight vessels, of all shapes and sizes, each and every day. An exception was in April 2016 when the canal had to remain closed for a week because of a drought resulting in the water being too low.

A couple of friends had told me how exciting they'd found it to travel through the canal on a cruise, the ship's sides barely able to squeeze through the locks on either side, consequently my visit to the Miraflores, a series of stepped locks where ships are lifted and lowered to pass through, was something I was looking forward to.

Sadly, my visit doesn't turn out as I'd hoped. At least it does, I do see the canal, but with no vessels in sight except for one tall ship which had completed the procedure just ten minutes before the visitor centre opened. It takes four hours to allow ships to pass through the Panama Canal before the directional flow is changed, as the system is one way only, meaning for that length of time there are no others being transported. And guess what, that's the time I'm here. With hindsight, it would have been better to have arranged my day's itinerary in a different order and visited the locks in the afternoon; I'm unsure why my guide hasn't planned it that way. However, I do get an idea of the scale of the manoeuvre, looking down over the lock and seeing how narrow the waterway actually is. Instead, I have to make do with the IMAX documentary at the visitor's centre to give me an understanding of how the locks work.

There's something else I want to do in Panama, if you've read about my visit to Peru, then you'll know I like to bring back Xmas presents for family from my trips. What better present than a genuine Panama hat. I explain to my guide what I'm looking to buy and ask him for a recommendation as to where I might shop for them. 'The old quarter is the best place,' he tells me, but first we drive out to a viewpoint by the marina. My guide explains the city is known as Little Miami or the Dubai of Central America; it makes sense looking at the cityscape across the water with its skyline of tall, modern buildings and knowing its popularity as a holiday destination, particularly for Americans. The place is heaving with them.

Later we pass a 'queue' of tankers and container ships out to sea which goes on for as far as the eye can see. 'These are the vessels waiting to travel through the Panama Canal,' my guide explains. 'They may have to wait days before it is their turn.' I'd had no idea of the size and scale of the traffic through the canal till then.

Driving here is manic with cars constantly changing lanes to get that one space ahead and doing so while their drivers are all on their phones. I'm relieved when we eventually manage to find a parking space, and I can get some respite.

The old quarter in Panama City, the part plundered by Henry Morgan in the seventeenth century then rebuilt in the colonial style, is my sort of place. Beautiful three storied buildings occupy the streets, with balconies and plants from hanging baskets draped prettily over the decorative iron balustrades. Many are colourfully painted. We visit San Jose church containing the largest Nativity scene I've ever come across. It takes up much of the space in the room and depicts how Bethlehem might have looked at the time of the birth of Christ; the houses, men and women going about their daily lives, the striped awnings of the bazaar, brightly coloured carpets on display, waiting to be sold, and at its centre the Nativity scene as we would recognise it. The attention to detail and intricacy of the design is amazing; another place I would have liked to have spent more time studying, but the number of people also wanting to look, make it impossible. Instead, we head outside and continue walking around.

My guide stops outside a shop on a nearby street corner. 'This is the best place for you to buy your hat.' The window is full of them; assorted colours, designs, shapes, and bands around the crown, including several types of Panamas.

The shop owner is very helpful and points me to a particular area of the shop where I can see what's on offer in the style I'm seeking. Whilst there are different shades, from white through to a beige, and different colour headbands, I'm after a traditional one, a pale cream with a black band. 'Which size do you want?' She asks. Mm, good question, I'm not sure. I decide on my size first and then think who else I want to get them for and try to work out sizes based on mine.

I say to my guide, 'Can you try one on please, to help me gauge which ones to get.' He dutifully tries on a few, but I'm still not sure. He is rather a large man but with a small head,

I'm even more uncertain but decide on two in the end and hope they'll fit.

The shop owner points out to me what a Panama should be like. 'It is made from a single toquilla palm and is handmade, you can see from the top of the crown how the hat has a circular weave, this is an indication of its authenticity.' Inside the hat she shows me more evidence of this. Stamped on the inner band it says, 'Montecristi, hand woven.' I have no idea of the significance. She tells me it is named after the city of the same name in Ecuador. I'm sceptical, I wanted to buy a genuine make, not one made in another country. The shop owner sees my hesitation and guesses why. 'Do you know proper Panama hats are all made in that country and the brand Montecristi is high end, the very best of Panamas. Feel how light it is, another indication of its provenance. You will not find a better quality anywhere,' she adds.

They are just what I wanted but I hesitate about buying more. 'Not sure how I'll get them home though,' I say.

She produces a flat box and explains, 'This will take up to eight hats.' She proceeds to carefully place one inside the other and expertly slides them in. I bite the bullet and decide to buy three more, five in total; I hope the sizes are right and what she's told me is true. All being well, that will be four Xmas presents taken care of plus one of the hats for me. I'm even more pleased when the price works out at twenty pounds cheaper than the ones I'd seen in M&S at home. They do look an excellent quality and also very classy. I'm relieved and a tad smug when I get back to my hotel and look up Montecristi Panamas on the internet. The shop owner hadn't been spinning me a yarn after all.

I make the choice to eat in the rooftop restaurant in the hotel this evening. I wouldn't normally have three courses, but the set menu sounds tempting, and it turns out to be the best meal I've had on my Central American trip so far. I start with melt in the mouth tortellini with a filling of roasted butternut squash and accompanied by a hazel, focaccia, and sage sauce. This is followed by linguini with beef and pork, all in a tasty pomodoro sauce, and then, if that wasn't enough, the dessert to finish is to die for, small parcels of pizza dough stuffed with Nutella and served with vanilla ice cream. All three courses were so light I don't feel too full at the end, and my glass of Chardonnay was pretty darned good as well.

I glance at the box of Panama hats sitting on the chair when I return to my room with a smile on my face, despite having missed out on seeing the Panama Canal in action. There is just one more day before I move onto my next country; I'm going to be spending it visiting the Embera Quera indigenous community on the Gatun River, and with it a chance to see another side of Panama.

My guide and I are dropped off at a patch of waste ground under a road bridge, there is only one other vehicle, a small coach which is empty, however I can hear excited voices chattering away up ahead. We walk towards the sounds and see a group of Japanese tourists by the river climbing into a long boat, sitting low in the water. At one end is a male youth dressed in nothing more than a brightly coloured loin cloth; he stands using a long wooden oar to steady the vessel. Soon it's my turn but I'm pleased to see my guide and I are the only ones occupying the next boat except for a second youth similarly attired in a loin cloth. He pushes his oar against the bank and we're off, gliding and being gently propelled along. I can hear the other group ahead, chatting to each other and I catch glimpses of them as we round a bend, but otherwise it's quiet, bar the sound of birdsong. The shrubbery along the riverbank is rich in greenness, creating reflections in the water and making it look an olive oil green colour, then the river narrows; reeds occupy the water on either side, and our boatman expertly uses his single oar to navigate us through the channel.

We come to a jetty where the passengers in the other boat are alighting, and we pull alongside. Up ahead I can see trees, manicured grass lawns, and large flowering bushes with bright pink flowers; it could be English parkland except for the seven conical shaped roofs made of thatch. We're taken to the largest of these, an open area with enough benches to house us all and greeted by five younger members of the community playing drums, a flute, and shakers. I wander over to the barbecue, drawn by the aroma of burning wood wafting around, and see a hive of activity; fillets of tilapia are grilling over the fire, lots of them, while to the side a long table is filled with bananas, pineapple, melon, mango and satsumas, all being prepared for our meal.

When lunch is brought to us, it is presented on two palm leaves; the top one is coiled round, creating a pocket for our fish with a wedge of lime to accompany it. The presentation would look good enough to grace any restaurant.

After more entertainment of singing and dancing, I'm pleased to report by both men and women, I take a stroll around. There is a primary school on site, however secondary school pupils have to take a boat ride to Panama City for their education. I notice brightly coloured strips of straw hanging out to dry and ask what they're used for. One of the community explains, 'They are stripped from palm leaves and used in basket making; lemon juice is used to dye them white, turmeric for yellow and iron root to get brown.' The shop has plenty of baskets made by the community for sale, but I resist, my Panama hats will have to do for now, as far as shopping is concerned.

It's time to leave; we make the same boat journey back, just the three of us again, me, my guide, and our helmsman, only this time I nearly lose my balance when my guide gets out of the boat and steps onto the riverbank. He is a tall, well-built man and his action causes the boat to rock from side to side. I could have done with a few heads to hold onto or helping hands, but I somehow manage to totter the length of the boat and make it safely back onto dry land.

I'd thought beforehand today's visit would give me an insight into what goes on beyond tourism and commerce, but there were around seventy visitors at the village and more arriving as I left. I wonder whether these tourist visits border on exploitation or, on the other hand, provide a source of income and are welcomed by the indigenous community. Not sure, and a little cynical, how authentic the experience was.

A small section of the Nativity scene in San Jose church

Gilberto takes us to his village Embera Quera

Guatemala

I can see a puff of smoke pluming from a volcano as we begin our descent, there is a sense of mystery about it; what lies below, what lies ahead of me on the next leg of my trip? We land in Antigua, pronounced with the sound of the 'u' included, unlike the island of the same name in the West Indies. It used to be the capital of Guatemala and the part of town where I'm staying was declared a world heritage site in the nineteen seventies.

My hotel, situated in the old quarter, is a boutique type, small and tastefully furnished; dark wooden furniture sits against whitewashed walls with huge bowls of white orchids lining the outside walkway to the reception area. My room is accessed via stepping stones laid in a shallow pool of water, right up to its door. I tread gingerly across and am thankful my suitcase is being carried by the person who greeted me on my arrival. He opens the door and places the suitcase just inside before handing me the key and leaving. It's a tiny space, the king-sized bed taking up most of it. The expression, 'Not big enough to swing a cat,' comes to mind, but it's gorgeous; there is a decorative iron bedstead and a white broderie anglaise cover draped over the bed, on one wall hang small oil paintings of South American figures in traditional dress and on another, wall hangings depicting Guatemalan culture. In the bathroom, dark wood beams support the ceiling, and a pretty porcelain basin sits on a stand. It is quaintly chic, and I love the room, despite its size.

I unpack what I can, storage space is limited and decide to have a recce round the town; the hotel doesn't have a restaurant, consequently finding somewhere to eat is a priority. My first impression of the town is that it has a laid-back feel; there are lots of hostels, laundry signs, small bars offering Happy Hour and tourists carrying large backpacks. I walk by brightly painted houses with iron grills in front of their windows and large wooden doors. The pavements are narrow and the kerbs steep, not good for my knees, and the roads are made up of rough cobblestones, not small round ones like I've seen in parts of other cities, but rectangular, uneven and larger, many of them with gaps between, making it easy, if one isn't careful, to turn an ankle. However, their primitive appearance only adds to the place's charm.

    I pass by restaurants and browse the menus as I go. In the end I choose one with an enclosed courtyard which doesn't look too busy. There are a couple of families finishing their lunch, it is late afternoon and too early still for the dinner clientele. It reminds me of Spain where I've often seen three or more generations gather to eat together; the children running around, whilst the adults relax and chat, with perhaps the odd reprimand to their offsprings, while the indulgent abuelas soothe and spoil their grandchildren.

    I choose a local dish, oxtail stew made with garlic, onions and a fruity broth of pineapple, tamarind, ginger, lime, and allspice. Not too filling but enough to satisfy my appetite. My dinner is completed with a Ferrero Rocher cornet.

    I stroll back to the hotel and carefully negotiate my way across the stepping stones to my room. A small parcel has been placed by my bedside, fastened with a miniature doll in traditional dress. In it I find two small macarons for my bedtime snack. A treatful way to end the day.

    My guide, German, pronounced Herman, is already in reception to greet me the next day. The first stop on our walking tour is to view the remains of San Jose Cathedral; much of it was destroyed by an earthquake in the eighteenth century, only some walls still exist, enough though to be able to imagine what it would have been like. The deep blue sky overhead peeps through the majestic structure of the roofless, cathedral creating shadows on the brick and stone walls, where in some parts the decorative markings can still be seen.

German tells me, 'In the last twenty-four hours there have already been nine rumblings from the active volcano nearby.' A scary thought. Evidently you can hike up another one next to it, camp overnight and look down into the active volcano to see the red glowing lava. The likelihood of an eruption is brought sharply into focus when German tells me that sometimes, if the activity is too fuerte, the airport is closed.

Our next visit is to the Convento de las Capuchinas (what a splendid name) and then onto the old public laundry, a place where women would gather to socialise, in addition to doing their washing. The open space in a small square with its row of stone sinks surrounding a central pool of water, still exists to this day, although only now as a tourist attraction.

Next, we visit a church to see how the Mayan culture was integrated after the Spanish invaded in the mid sixteenth century. German explains, 'To keep the indigenous Mayan people on its side, the Catholic church incorporated some of their symbols into religious buildings.' He points out a stuccoed cocoa plant above the entrance then shows me an artefact of the Virgin Mary inside with a moon representing fertility in the Mayan culture at its base. In the next few days, I'll see more examples of how Mayan beliefs still exist as an integral part of Guatemala.

I'm hot and tired by the end of the tour and remember that my hotel has an arrangement with another close by with a pool. I can't think of anything more welcoming at that moment than a chance to swim and relax. It is bliss, and later, I make the choice to return to the same hotel for dinner. There is a Valentine's Day floral photo booth in the entrance to the bar with a sign above saying, 'Better Together.' It's easy to lose track of the date when I'm away, and I work out I've already been on my trip for seventeen days. How time flies.

My cocktail challenge for this trip has been neglected for a while; I've tried about eight so far but have asked my WhatsApp followers to suggest a few. My list to date includes Cosmopolitan, Daiquiri with mango, Screwdriver, Guaro Sour, Pina Colada, Tamarindo Sunrise, Mai Thai and Laguna Azul. A suggestion comes back from a friend, Negroni, equal measure of Campari, red vermouth, and gin. None of this added fruit juice malarkey, now that's what I call a cocktail.

After an enjoyable meal and the Negroni, I return to my hotel and find another goodie bag has been left in my room with a miniature doll attached; this time there are cookies inside. With three young grandchildren back in England, I'm hoping another doll tomorrow night will give me one to take home for each of them.

Breakfast is on the roof the next day, there is no-one around when I get there, but I don't have to wait long before the server arrives to take my order. I choose an acai green bowl, mashed avocado, oats, pumpkin seeds, apple, mango and acai, and a freshly squeezed orange juice. It is refreshing and set me up perfectly for my busy day; I have a cooking class arranged for the morning followed by a rum tasting in the afternoon, two additions to my itinerary which I'd booked independently via the website, Trip Advisor.

The roads in the old town are so uneven that for much of the getting around, tuk tuks are used instead of cars. A beaten up looking one arrives to collect me for my cooking class, driven by a young man who hardly looks old enough to be driving. I hop in and hold on for dear life as the vehicle bumps and speeds its way through the cobbled streets. What can I say about the experience except that I feel like a dry martini cocktail in a Bond film by the time we reach our destination, vigorously shaken rather than stirred.

My fellow classmates, seven of them, are already there; they come from different countries, but all speak English. We nod and say hello to each other before our two hosts take over and explain what we're going to cook. First, we all have a try at making tortillas for the dobladas. 'Don't add so much water,' I'm told by one of our hosts, when mine don't work out as they should. He explains, 'That's why it's sticking.' After another try, I give up gracefully and leave it to those with more expertise and instead turn my hand to other chores. We chop, slice, and mix to prepare the toppings and then stand back to admire our creations. The dobladas are now covered with guacamole, chopped radishes, tomato and tomato salsa, sliced onion, parsley, and a salty cheese. Next, we make rellenitos by first mashing boiled plantain with cinnamon, rolling it into a ball, then hollowing out the centre and filling them with a chocolate and bean sauce, before they're fried. As you can imagine, by this time, I'm salivating.

When all the preparations have been finished, we sit down round a table laid out on the terrace and enjoy the dobladas we made, passing dishes between us and diving in.

We wait awhile, swapping stories about our holidays while the main course, Pepiyan, finishes cooking. One couple say their main reason for coming to Antigua was to do the hike up the volcano and camp at the top. They say how jaw dropping the moment was when they looked down into the other volcano and saw it gurgling away. Any extra tours I book like this give me the chance to spend time with others and hear about the experiences they've had, bringing yet another dimension to my travel adventures.

The chicken stew when it arrives is juicy and flavoursome but I'm not too enamoured with the rellenitos, which we'd made to accompany it, a little dry for my liking.

I have a few hours before I have to walk the short distance to Casa del Ron, the rum distillery, later this afternoon. Spending the time by the pool is inviting so I go for a swim in the nearby hotel again, then relax on my sun lounger, fascinated by the small white puffs of smoke I can see being emitted at regular intervals from the top of the active volcano.

The tasting isn't what I expect, for a start it's just me. I'm presented with tasting notes and invited to sit down in a large, leather armchair while my rum is sorted. It comes on a wooden tray with three glasses, each one containing a generous measure, and with it there are nibbles placed between the glasses, indicating the order I should eat them in: a salty cracker, three roasted almonds and a chocolate.

I had no idea beforehand that rum has the complexities of something like brandy, my eyes are being opened. My notes say smoky amongst other things for the first one, I take a whiff and enjoy the aroma, then a taste. Mm, very easy to drink, however I take my time. A humidor room is a metre away to my left, no doubt containing a wide selection of cigars. It's over forty years since I gave up smoking, but I like the image which has just appeared in my mind of me sitting here sipping my rum, while puffing on a cigar.

One glass down, two to go; I cleanse my palate with the cracker and a few mouthfuls of water then pick up the second glass. My tasting notes tell me to compare the colour of the three rums before I try them, all three are different shades of rich brown, I'm guessing affected by how long they have been distilled and in which type of cask. I recall many years ago, going on a sherry tour to the Williams and Humbert Bodega in Jerez, the company which produces Dry Sac. We were told how the casks storing the sherry can influence the taste, and I know that's true of wine as well.

This rum seems fruitier than the first, although not sweet. Again, I allow my tastebuds to savour the taste and try to decide which one of the two I prefer, but they are both very pleasing and I can't choose. The three almonds help me cleanse my palate again before I pick up the last glass. It is much darker and richer in aroma, and my notes say caramel and molasses, also aged for much longer. Again, I take my time, aware I still have to negotiate the uneven cobblestones and steep kerbs, not to mention the stepping stones across water to my hotel room. The whole tasting experience has been an eye opener and very enjoyable. I'll definitely buy a bottle of rum at the airport when I've finished my trip, however, I still have a way to go on my itinerary before then.

The next day I choose the red acai bowl for breakfast and wonder why I'm not making something like this at home. Pureed raspberry, strawberries, oats, pumpkin seeds, almonds, and acai make a great start to today.

German and I are moving on; the car journey is only two and half hours but seems longer. We eventually reach our destination, Lake Atitlan, by mid afternoon. The writer, Aldous Huxley described it as the most beautiful lake in the world, and it certainly does look stunning. The lake is the deepest one in the whole of Central America and was formed by a volcano erupting. It now sits on its crater and is surrounded by six other volcanoes, two of which are still active.

All the rooms in the hotel have balconies overlooking the lake; I sit on mine and enjoy the glorious view, watching the stream of boats pulling in and out of the jetties, transporting locals and tourists alike. The water is a deep grey blue except for the wake created by the boats, and it is relatively peaceful despite the constant traffic on the water.

We visit the vast Chichicastenango market the next day, it appears and disappears twice a week and has existed for hundreds of years. For anyone looking for souvenirs to take home, it is a shoppers' paradise. Having said that it's also a place where local inhabitants come to shop. German shows me how it really is a pop-up market with waste bins on poles which retract into the ground. He takes me around, pointing out different things as we stroll; children making tortillas to sell, makeshift stoves to cook them on, more varieties of corn than I could ever have imagined, babies and toddlers aplenty, huddled in papooses made of colourful fabric across their mothers' backs. We come to a square where a church service has just taken place and the congregation is spilling out. Many of the congregation are wearing traditional Guatemalan clothing, the men in white shirts and black trousers with colourful hats on, the women in bright dresses and straw hats. So nice to be surrounded by the happenings of the community.

It isn't this spectacle but another at the church in the centre of the market which moves me more. Of all the religious buildings I've ever visited in my whole life, what I see here is something which has a profound effect. Santo Tomaso, at the centre of the market, is a Catholic church built on the site of an ancient Mayan temple; the original rough hewn dark steps up to the entrance still exist, here two people are partaking in Mayan rituals. I watch as they light vessels then wave incense in front of the entrance as an offering to the gods. One of them takes a bottle of rum and sprinkles some of the contents on the step into the church itself, again as an offering. It seems odd to see this in front of a Catholic church but at the same time, strangely beautiful, the two religions working in harmony with one another.

Inside I see another form of worship, two women are shuffling on their knees the thirty or so metres to the altar, each one carrying a bunch of flowers as their offering. It is dramatic, and the simple interior of the church only adds to the poignancy of their action. I find the spectacle very moving for some reason, the two religions working in the same space, their followers worshipping in their own way.

German takes me to a room above a shop; he explains the importance of festivals in Guatemala and shows me the highly decorative costumes, embellished with gold and silver braid, used in theatre dance, and worn during the parades. 'Would you like to try one of them on?' He asks. In for a penny in for a pound, I think, why not? The jacket, trousers and headdress feel heavy when I put them on, but I decline wearing the mask as well. I pose while he takes a photo for me. One definitely for the memory bank!

I'm left to wander around for an hour, and I can't stop taking photos, the abundance of colour is out of this world. There are bags of all shapes and sizes, clothing, throws, wall hangings, it goes on and on. I stand and admire a stall with women's beautiful, patterned jackets on display, and compliment the man selling them. He tells me they are his handiwork. I succumb and decide to buy one in peacock blue with front panels decorated in patterns using pink, yellow and red. It will be another special memory of my time here whenever I wear it.

I've been searching for a cushion cover to go with the two cushions I have at home from Vietnam and South Africa. My lounge already contains a number of objects from my travels, a bonsai sculpture from an Arizona flea market, and a hardanger embroidery from Canada, among others. I enjoy having memories of places I've visited around me. In the end I buy a small sampler to create a panel on a plain cushion cover I have at home. The design is more Aztec but in muted shades of beige and green and will fit perfectly with the colours in my lounge.

By this time, I'm in need of a sit down and find a café with a small outdoor seating area. I order my cappuccino, feeling pleased with my wares and ask the two young women occupying the only other table if one of them would mind taking my photo. We have a brief conversation; they are from Sweden and backpacking their way around. 'You're travelling alone?' They ask in astonishment. I nod my head. 'We admire you,' they add. I feel flattered; there's nothing like a compliment to bolster you.

My meal this evening is at one of the many restaurants along the lake shore. I watch the boats still criss crossing the lake to drop off at anyone of the twenty towns and villages surrounding the water. I'm pleased to report though there isn't a party boat in sight. My meal of fajitas isn't brilliant but edible. I sit and think about what the two Swedish women had said. Yes, coming here on a five-week trip alone is pretty amazing. It's one of those odd moments when I feel proud of myself.

The next day we take a ride to visit two towns across the lake. The boat crashes in and out of the waves, creating a banging sound every time it does so; not what one would describe as a smooth journey, but we arrive in one piece at our first stop, San Juan. I have a funny moment when I have to climb out of the boat onto the jetty, a good metre higher than where I'm standing. With the help of German on one side of me and the boat driver on the other, I manage it, somehow finishing standing on my feet rather than belly flopping onto the wooden walkway which I'd envisaged. The town stretches upwards ahead of me, and it looks like its going to be a steep walk, however German urges me to take my time and stop if I need to. The altitude is around fifteen hundred metres he tells me, a doddle I think to myself, I managed over four thousand in Peru. Nevertheless, I take the opportunity to pause and look at the many souvenir shops lining our route just in case my breathing gets difficult. There is a feast of colour and pattern wherever I look.

Away from the quayside and souvenir shops, it is quieter; a number of houses still maintain the kaleidoscope of colour which appears to be a feature of Guatemala, their brightly painted walls festooned with murals. German tells me it is where his home is and where he grew up. 'Do you get back home often?' I ask.

'Yes, when the tourist season is over but only the odd time apart from then.' Well, at least tonight he'll have the chance to be with his family.

We enter a shop, and I watch a dyeing and weaving demonstration before buying a couple of bumbags for my grandchildren. Purple seems to be the in colour with them both, so I choose two but with different patterns on; I'm hoping they'll like them when I get back home.

Our next port of call is Santiago, another town bordering Lake Atitlan. It is more run down and less tourist oriented than San Juan, with only a handful of souvenir shops near the jetty area, however what I'm about to see beggars belief. We alight the boat and walk up the main drag before cutting down an alleyway; I wonder where on earth I'm being taken. German leads me into the back entrance of a house where a man sits next to what I can only describe as the figure of an ugly cowboy look alike, including the hat. A smoking cigar is coming out of his mouth, the figure's not the man's. My eyes must have spoken volumes but before German has a chance to explain, a man appears from outside and places money on the lap of the figure. He bends in front of it and mutters something then leaves as swiftly as he has come. The cowboy's 'guardian' immediately removes the money and stuffs it in his pocket. German explains, 'This figure represents the god Maximon, he is an important part of the spirituality and beliefs of the Mayans. People come here to pay homage to him.' I sit in silence as more people enter and follow the same ritual. I can't get my head round the fact that an effigy looking like a seedy cowboy, smoking a cigar, in the back room of a pretty ordinary house, is sitting a couple of metres away and being worshipped as a deity. It all seems very strange, but then a well-known hymn does say, 'God moves in mysterious ways, his wonders to perform.' Who am I to judge?

I'm ready to put my feet up by the time we return to the hotel, having walked ten kilometres today according to my health app and climbed the equivalent of sixteen floors. However, I still enjoy a quick swim in the pool to cool me off. Having had lunch out, I decide to skip dinner and sit on my balcony instead, watching the twinkling lights come on over the lake from the different communities across the water. Think I'll sleep well tonight.

Today, I'm leaving Lake Atitlan, but first, on the way to the airport, there is one more place to visit. We stop at Iximche at Tecpan, the first of the four Mayan sites I'll be seeing on my trip. The city was the first capital of Guatemala until the Spanish invaded and was built as late as the fifteenth century. The next three sites are much older, German tells, me, but better preserved, however this one will give me a flavour of what's in store when I move on.

At Iximche, we come across a man standing by a small fire; he is conducting a Mayan ritual, not dissimilar to the one I saw outside the church at Chichicastenango, offering smoke to the gods. Beer is being poured on this time, rather than rum, again as an offering. This sort of practice was banned by the Catholic church until the late twentieth century but now is widespread. German assures me, the ritual is not in any way done as a tourist attraction but just as part of the community's life.

I'm at the airport now for my flight to the north of the country, to Flores, visiting the second of the Mayan citadels, this one in the jungle. Bug spray and sun lotion will need to be slathered on for sure. I say my goodbyes to German and thank him for his brilliant guiding over the past seven nights; his excellent knowledge has given me a valuable insight into the country's heritage and beliefs. He is heading straight back to Antigua to pick up his next tourists. No rest for the wicked.

I have a long wait at the airport, and, because of its size, there is little to see or do. I get out my tablet and spend the time writing. I'm in the middle of a fiction; not something to explain about now other than to say I've come to enjoy putting pen to paper recently and immerse myself in a couple of hours of indulgence, only to find later my tablet hasn't saved it and I've lost a couple of thousand words. Another reminder to myself on this trip to double check everything.

My plane when we walk out of the departure lounge looks like a throwback to the nineteen sixties; I can remember as teenager flying to Spain in something similar on BEA, if any of you are old enough to remember that airline. Do modern planes have propellers now? Nevertheless, it does get me to my destination in one piece.

It was dark when I arrived at my hotel the night before, and the song My Way was being belted out in a nearby bar, but with my trusty earplugs in place, I managed a good night's sleep. And here I am the next day, bright eyed and bushy tailed, ready for the off. I don't have to wait long before Juan, my guide, arrives to meet me and take me to Tikal.

We stop off at the visitors' centre and look at a model of the national park to give me an overview; it is another UNESCO World Heritage site and the largest excavated one in the Americas, covering two hundred square miles.

Juan leads me to the outdoor area and points out different shrubs and trees of interest. First, he shows me an allspice tree with its patchy bark. I'd always thought allspice was a sort of hybrid; a mix of cloves, cinnamon et cetera, but no, much to my surprise, it really does exist. We move to another shrub; this time I recognise it straightaway; the large yellowy brown pods hold cocoa beans, used to make a whole variety of chocolate related products. Mm, fancy growing one of those in your back garden.

'Do you know what this tree is called?' Juan asks, moving on to another one. I shake my head. 'Sapodilla,' he declares. I'm still in the dark. 'A chewing gum tree.' I'm reminded of an April Fool's Day prank on TV about the spaghetti tree and wait for an explanation. He explains, 'The Mayans had been chewing on chicle, the gum from the tree, for centuries then along came the Wrigley company, added flavouring and sugar to the substance, and the rest is history. My, my, what a lot I'm learning on this trip.

We're dropped off at the entrance to Tikal and Juan goes to sort out our tickets. 'The bus to take us to the first site will be another twenty minutes. We can wait or walk, whichever you prefer,' he explains on his return. It is hot already, despite the early hour, but I decide walking will give me a better feel of the place. The decision is a good one; the trees lining our route offer plenty of shade, I can hear birds above me and monkeys moving about nearby. We stop at the base of a tall tree where a few people are gathered, looking upwards. I think they must have spotted a monkey, but no they haven't, they're looking at the tree itself. 'This is a kapok tree,' Juan explains. 'Look, can you see the large balls of fluff on the branches? The wind will blow them down and then they are collected for production.' Yet another first for me on this trip. I had no idea where kapok came from, only that my mum used to buy it to stuff the knitted dolls she made.

We walk on and suddenly a clearing appears in front of me, and there it is, my first real look at the distinctive pyramid shape of a Mayan temple. This site was only rediscovered by missionaries and local people in the nineteenth century; can you imagine what it would have been like to come across these structures in the middle of a north Guatemalan jungle? What a spectacle it must have been when they were originally built, painted red, a colour associated with life (blood) and in Mayan beliefs, the middle world.

We carry on and before long come to another, it's like being in the Raiders of The Lost Ark movie, surrounded by trees one minute then in a clearing the next, these magnificent structures appearing out of nowhere. In fact, I discover later the location was used for one of the Stars Wars films.

The third one we come to has a wooden staircase behind it and the chance to climb to the top. 'What do you think, would you like to see from the top?' Juan asks. He looks at me benignly, expecting me to refuse. I'm a little put out by his assumption that at my age I wouldn't want to do it, but my inner youth takes over and belligerence eggs me on to reply.

'Yes, definitely.' Although it's a long way to the top, the staircase is easy to climb, and I manage it without having to stop. I look over the canopies of trees and see two, three, four temples peeping through, evidently one of them is seventy metres high and is the tallest pre-Colombian structure in all the Americas.

When my guide catches me up, he says, 'You are very fit.' I'm tempted to explain that his scepticism was the thing which motivated me. There's nothing like a challenge to spur me on. I know my ageing knees won't always see me through but there's still life in this old dog, and unlike Peru and Bolivia, I don't have the problem of high altitude to cope with.

I return to my hotel later and marvel at what I've seen and learned today; a feast of facts and sights for me to assimilate.

The bar in the early evening is quiet, and it's been a good few days since I added to my cocktail list. I peruse what's on offer from the bar menu; some unusual choices, one of which was my dad's favourite, Carajillo, although never made with the liqueur Cuarenta Tres and never as a cocktail. It would be his daily midmorning drink on holiday, expresso and brandy served in a small tumbler sitting on a saucer.

One of my WhatsApp friends had suggested that to help me decide which cocktail to order, I should ask the bartender for a recommendation, and so I do. His choice is Naba-Cuc, (no, I'd never heard of it either); gin, pimiento, and tamarind juice with a long slice of cucumber lining the bottom and sides of the bowl-shaped glass. I take a sip and find it on the bitter side. Not my favourite but certainly different, and one more to add to my list for the trip.

The next morning offers me the chance to look round, I'm staying in the historic old town of Isla de Flores, positioned in the middle of a small lake. It has a Caribbean feel, and every building is painted in bright colours. My hotel has an exterior with an attractive floral outline painted on the cream walls in jade, a favourite colour of mine, the doors leading out onto the verandas are in the same colour as are the iron railings on each balcony; it's the prettiest looking hotel I've ever stayed in. I wander through the cobblestone streets, taking photos as I go, browsing in the odd shop, and feeling chilled.

Before I know it, my taxi is here to take me onto the next leg of my journey. It's time to say goodbye to Guatemala, to its smiley, friendly people (everyone says Buenos Dias and looks at you when they say it), glorious colour, and pride in the Mayan heritage. I've loved my time here and would definitely recommend it. However, there is a new experience waiting for me on my travels. Today I cross the land border into Belize, the fourth of my five countries. A mere ten more days to go before my trip comes to an end, where has the time gone, but until then, there are plenty more cocktails to try!

Antigua old town with active volcano

Madonna with moon Mayan symbol at base

Everyday wear for the market

Mayan ritual performed at Iximche

Carnival time in Chichicastenango

Belize

The land border where I'm dropped off looks run down; it seems strange to be crossing into another country on foot. The entrada takes me into a long room, more like a corridor, with an entrance at one end and the exit at the other with little else between except a table on one side and two enclosed Perspex booths on the other. In one of them sits a man waiting to 'greet' me. I assume this is passport control and hand him my passport. He takes it from me, has a cursory glance, gives me a form to fill in, and waves me away without speaking a word. I point to my passport, but he shakes his head, places it to the side of him and shoos me away angrily. I don't like the idea of not having it on my person but have to do as he commands. An English couple, the only other people in the room, kindly lend me a pen, (why do always forget to keep one on my person) and I dutifully do as I've been instructed. I search through my paperwork for the address of the lodge where I'll be staying but without success; it's not on my itinerary and without internet connection, I'm unable to find it. Is this going to be a problem, I ask myself, especially given the almost hostile manner of the person who will decide whether to let me into the country. I return to where he is sitting, point to the relevant space on the form and apologise. 'Lo siento.' I'm intimidated and can feel myself getting hotter, but he exasperatedly shakes his head, mutters something and aggressively stamps my passport. My first experience of Belize isn't a pleasant one, nevertheless, I'm here, unharmed.

A few weeks before the start of my trip, I'd received an email from my travel company saying a mistake had been made and I would have to stay at the lodge where I'm now heading, for an extra night. I'd been sceptical about this part of the itinerary and had already questioned it; not that I have anything against lodges per se, having already stayed in one in South Africa and Borneo, but, unlike those, this one didn't offer much that appealed to me. The planned two nights there would have meant one and half days at the lodge, but three nights would add a whole extra day. There seemed to be no alternative, so I had reluctantly agreed to go along with it. Maybe it wouldn't be as bad as I'd imagined, I'd told myself.

As it turns out, the lodge is everything I was dreading. The person who greets me in reception takes me into the large open-sided communal area and explains the meal situation. She tells me guests are limited to only one plate of food at breakfast, that tea and coffee are served at mealtimes but otherwise I could purchase them. I think to myself, that's okay, I can make myself a cup in my room. A dream!

The optional activities are explained to me; guided hikes through the jungle to see birds, flora and fauna, and river tubing (but not at the moment because the water is too low). I'd read about this before I came and it sounded fun until it's then explained to me how I would have to collect my tube, take a twenty minute walk through the jungle to the start, (carrying my tube), and then the whole process repeated if I want to give it another go. Not the most appealing sounding activity for me. I'm told there is also a pool or the river to swim in, or I could sit and birdwatch. Feeders have been put out around the communal area to attract the birds, and I notice a pretty black and white one with a bright red patch on its head as we're talking. Unbelievably cute but not my sort of thing for any length of time. 'Internet is fine here in the communal space but as your room isn't near the main hub, connection isn't good,' my greeter goes on to explain. The alarm bells in my head are getting louder.

'Let me get someone to show you to your room,' she says. I count the steps as we descend, eighty in all. My stay is becoming less and less appealing. On the trek to my room, we pass the pool, probably no more than three metres long; so much for me thinking I might spend some of the time swimming.

I have to admit, my room, when we eventually reach it, is pleasant enough with modern furnishings and a spacious outside veranda, however there is no coffee and tea making facility, and the view of the river, a muddy greyish beige colour, makes swimming unappealing. I can't imagine myself staying here; no hot drinks or internet, no-one to chat to except at mealtimes, and eighty steps to climb up and down whenever I want any of those. This must all sound terribly negative, and I'm sure the feeling of isolation would appeal to some but for two and a half days, no, this wasn't for me.

I decide that I'll have to put the whole episode down to experience, to accept things don't always go exactly as you want them to. I'll learn from it and resolve to be more insistent in the future about what I do or don't like on my itinerary. To cut a long story short, I contact the travel agent and am removed to a hotel nearby for one night, somewhere I could sit in a lounge area and people watch or retire to my room and make a nice cup of tea.

By early evening I'm hungry, the restaurant menu in the hotel is horrendously expensive, however, I'd noticed a dodgy looking casino along the road when we arrived, so I venture out to see if it has an eatery inside. I've only ever been to a casino once and that was fifty years ago.

'Are you a member?' I'm asked. 'You have to be a member to use the casino.'

'Oh,' I reply, feeling somewhat dejected. My stomach is telling me I must eat and soon.

'But you can join today, it's free and you'll have life membership.'

I dutifully fill in the form and am given a membership card; in no time at all I'm sitting down enjoying a tasty plate of nachos. And if, in the unlikely chance I ever go back to that particular town in Belize, my life membership will allow me to go play the tables!

I'm moving on to Ambergris Cay, the next place on my itinerary, a day early but before then my guide takes me on an extra excursion to Barton Creek, by way of apology for the inconvenience I've been caused. We climb into a canoe and paddle our way towards the cavernous opening ahead; the underground waterway was once a sacred ceremonial site for the Mayans, the high walls, fascinating rock formations, and provenance giving it a sense of mysticism.

As if that wasn't enough, there is a chance to do zip wiring again. I feel more confident this time as I'm belted up and taken to the first starting point. The seven lines seem to flash by in an instant and as with the previous occasion, at the end, I wish I could do it all over again. My guide returns my camera; because it was only the two of us on this occasion, he was able to capture me on video. Definitely Nana points with the grandchildren.

Belize City is crowded and noisy. I've been driven here to take a boat across to Ambergris Cay, Belize's largest island, for a couple of days of rest and relaxation. Little has happened on my itinerary in this country so far because of the lodge debacle, nevertheless I'm looking forward to my first visit to the Caribbean. We get to the port early and see a long queue waiting for the boat before mine. My driver explains that when the passengers start to board, I should immediately join the new line. He says, 'You will have to wait about forty minutes before your boat is ready to board but the queues get long very quickly.' I people watch, unsure whether I want to lug my suitcase to browse round the souvenir shops. I have an enjoyable book to read and plenty of music to listen to, so I sit out the wait, all the time keeping a watchful eye on the queue.

Eventually the line begins to move, and I gather my stuff ready to start forming a new one. I have a sudden thought, will there be a loo on board, the bane of my life as I've gotten older? I decide not to take the chance and go before joining the line. I realise on my return the mistake I've made, by now the newly formed queue has about eighty people in front of me, and the previous boat hadn't looked that big. I stand there, ticket in hand as more people filter in behind me; I'm hoping more tickets wouldn't have been sold if there wasn't adequate space.

After what seems like a long time, the queue starts to move, and as I edge forward I can see the boat is looking pretty full already. Somehow, to my relief, we are all squeezed on board, a kind young woman stands and offers me her seat, and we're off. The boat picks up speed and heads out to sea, the sun is setting, reflecting across the water, and turning the sky into a glorious golden yellow before dark descends. I think about the last couple of days and what a disappointment they've been and then followed by the drive to the capital and the arduous wait for the boat. I grunt and remind myself, well you wanted adventure Jan, didn't you? Life is all about experiences and whilst this wasn't the most pleasant of ones, I'm still alive, I didn't come to any harm and I'm in one piece. Nothing else could possibly go wrong now………….or could it?

I step onto the jetty at San Pedro, the island's main town, with suitcase and backpack in hand and see a row of golf buggies waiting, their drivers holding cards with passengers' names on. However, I don't see one for me. It's been a long day, and I just want to get to my hotel. The jetty gradually empties as the golf buggies depart, taking the various visitors off to their accommodations, and I'm left alone, except for two men standing and chatting idly about ten metres away. I look up the beach and can see no-one else. What to do, surely someone will be here soon to take me to my hotel, what else could go wrong today? Should I ask these two complete strangers for help, is that wise? All these thoughts are going through my head. One of the men says goodbye to his companion and departs, leaving just the two of us. So here I am, alone in a foreign country, it is deserted, dark, I don't know where I'm going and I'm not liking the feel of Belize at all. 'Excuse me,' I say hesitantly, approaching the man and pulling my suitcase behind me. He turns and I see in front of me an Ainsley Herriot look alike, with the same huge smile and as tall, but considerably wider.

He asks in a laid-back Caribbean accent, 'Hello, welcome to San Pedro, I'm Tony, what is your name?'

I normally call myself Jan, but I've found on this holiday it has been misheard as Jane, Jean and even John. So, I reply, 'Janis.'

Tony gives out a loud belly laugh and says, 'Janis Green!' I do a double take, how can he possibly know my birth name, is this some kind of joke? Is it on my passport and the travel company looking after me here has somehow gotten my name muddled up? 'Janis Green,' he repeats, chuckling and shaking his head in surprise. 'That is the name of my mum's best friend in England. In Coventry,' he explains. 'Have you ever met her?' By now I'm bordering on hysteria, what with the chain of events in the last couple of days and now this. He directs my attention along the beach when I ask him if my hotel is far from here. 'About three hundred metres that way,' he explains. 'I'll take you, let me have your case.'

I'm reluctant, after all, this man could be anybody. 'No, it's okay, I can manage.'

He walks me up the beach to the road, points me in the right direction, shakes my hand, and says, 'Goodbye Janis Green.' I can still hear his laughter as I set off on my way to find the hotel. What a coincidence eh.

When I tell this story to my WhatsApp group later, my friend replies, 'Better not to get picked up and sent to a harem.' At my age? Come on, who are you kidding? Although, I guess I could count it as another adventure!

My accommodation is for one night before I move to the hotel in my booking. It's in a block of apartments and at first glance, I think I could comfortably stay here for the whole of my visit. There is a lounge and kitchen as well as bedroom and bathroom, and attached to the apartments is a bar restaurant with an outdoor eating area which looks out to sea. I decide a large alcoholic drink is what's needed and try a recommendation from the bartender. It's delicious; banana liqueur, white rum, coconut rum, orange juice, and grenadine.

A woman sitting at the bar starts up a conversation with me, she is American and is staying in the block of apartments next to mine. She leaves her husband at home a couple of times a year and comes here by herself to snorkel. We chat for a while before she returns to her apartment, and I'm left to have a look at the menu. I order comfort food, burger, fries, and salad, then move to sit at a table from where I can look out over the water. Bliss!

There is no-one about at the apartments when I emerge from my room the next day. I pass by the small kidney shaped swimming pool and smile at one of the rules displayed on a notice. 'No prancing permitted in the pool,' it says. I'm not sure what that means, but it amuses me anyway. Visions of synchronised swimming come to my mind first, then of horses being put through their paces in a dressage sequence in the water; the images are all a little surreal. I cross the veranda where I'd eaten the previous evening, open the gate and step onto the boardwalk to take an early morning amble and get my bearings. There is a beautiful stillness about the sea, and the comfortably warm air temperature makes for pleasant walking.

Everyone I meet is smiling and greets me with a 'Beautiful morning,' or 'Fine day it's going to be.' Suddenly a voice booms out behind me, 'Janis Green!' It's Tony, my newfound buddy. I explain why I was hesitant to let him help me the day before, however he shakes his head and tells me the reason I needn't have worried. 'The British used to have an army base in Belize, many expats married local Belizeans and settled here. Everyone on the cay loves people from the UK.' I thank him again for his kindness. I can still hear him muttering to himself, 'Janis Green,' as he walks away. I didn't like to tell him there is a third one I know of, by virtue of the fact I share the same Christian name as my sister-in-law, although spelt differently, and being married to my brother, her surname is Green too.

There are restaurants spaced at intervals along the beach and restauranteurs are busy already writing their menus on big blackboards; one sign says lobster in citric garlic butter, touch of white wine and steamed veggies, while another may not sound quite as classy, but is way more eclectic; lobster burrito, fettucine, empanadas, chowder, fajitas, fritters, burgers, ceviche, BBQ, curried and fried, would you believe. If only I liked the taste of lobster.

After a hearty breakfast, I take another walk but this time away from the beach area and find myself in a busy part of town. Here, traffic is noisy; golf buggies vie with cars and motor bikes for space on the narrow roads, locals and tourists jostle with each other to pass along the pavements, and it is hot and dusty.

I feel the need for something to cool and soothe me and buy a green smoothie from a street corner booth where a young woman stands idly behind the counter, looking bored. There is nowhere to sit so I stand under the shade by the counter and enjoy my drink. A couple walk by and then turn back to look at the list of choices hanging on a sign above. I strike up conversation. 'This one's lovely,' I tell them. 'It took me a while to decide which to have because they all sound so delicious.' The couple make their choices and wait with me till theirs have been prepared. By the time I finish my drink, there are another three people, all tourists, waiting. Funny how a queue attracts buyers. Perhaps I should have asked for commission.

I browse in the odd shop as I walk around but am not tempted to buy anything; everything appears to be super expensive, especially after the market prices in Guatemala.

In the evening, I take another stroll along the boardwalk to seek out an Italian restaurant I'd passed on my walk in the morning. There are people along the beach at the ends of the numerous jetties, from where, in the morning, small boats carrying snorkellers will set off for the reef. They sit on their chairs, gazing out to sea and idly chatting away in their Caribbean accent, while the water laps gently below them. Their chilled, laidback way of talking and moving captures the ambience of the place perfectly.

The restaurant is busy; a group of young men with loud voices in an American accent are obviously having a suitable time. I'm guessing they're on a stag do or maybe just a friend's jolly. I would describe them as preppy; Ralph Lauren polo shirts, chinos, or Bermudas, sockless and wearing loafers. One is speaking on his phone, trying to arrange a fleet of golf buggies to take them goodness knows where. I think they'll probably leave soon but another round of cocktails is brought to their table. Their noisy exuberance is too much for me. I eat my lasagne quickly and return my apartment.

The next day I change accommodation to a resort which is obviously geared up for the American tourist market. It isn't so much my sort of place as the apartments, but I do have a spacious chalet, including a balcony and view of the sea.

Again, I take a walk away from the beach after breakfast and find a roadside booth; the only wares for sale seem to be a few vegetables, however there is a fridge with a selection of cold drinks in. A teenager and an older lady are doing the selling, (please note, I refuse to call her old, although she looks well into her eighties. It's all relative isn't it.) I buy four bottles of coke, considerably cheaper here than in the hotel. The octogenarian holds up four fingers, indicating the price for them all. I give her a five US dollar note but forget two

Belize dollars are equivalent to one US dollar. She looks at me in surprise when I tell her to keep the change. I realise afterwards her prices are probably in Belize, so my tip of three US dollars, if you could call it that, was a tad generous to say the least.

My full intentions are to snorkel while I'm here, the coral reef is second only in size to the Great Barrier Reef in Australia, but I find myself getting irrationally nervous at the thought. Images of sharks appear in my mind and of my breathing being restricted with my snorkel on. (I've not done any since I was a child and then only in shallow water). I find myself fretting, umming and ahing whether I should do it. No matter how much I try to convince myself the sharks aren't dangerous, I'd prefer to do a bungee jump than get into shark infested waters. I wish I could be braver and just go but I can't, and realise worrying about it is spoiling my visit. I cop out in the end, and know I might regret my decision, but for the moment it's the right one for me. Sadly, the alternative of a trip in a glass bottomed boat isn't possible because the only one in the town is out of action for maintenance.

Nearly five weeks since I left home, perhaps all the travelling is catching up with me, maybe that's the reason for my lack of umph. Instead, I spend the afternoon lounging on the beach, watching the sun peep through the palm trees, dipping my toes in the sea, and listening to my Latin funk playlist. Later, I sit in a hammock and watch the sunset, giving myself permission to accept turning down a challenge. There will be more adventures another time, of that I'm sure.

On my day of departure, I'm driven by golf buggy to the other side of the cay to catch a boat for my journey to the fifth and final country of my trip, Mexico, and the chance to discover more about the Mayans. My time in Belize has been mixed, some good and some not so good, but I try to think of the positives; I've visited a new country, recharged my batteries, and you never know, one day in the future, I might get to Coventry and meet my namesake.

My second zip wiring experience

Barton Creek ancient Mayan burial site

Lobster with everything in this restaurant

Mexico

The boat for the ninety-minute journey to Mexico is much smaller than the one which brought me to Belize, and there are only a handful of passengers. I get talking to a young Dutch woman who tells me she's just spent two months travelling through Colombia. She says what a wonderful country it is, and I wonder how safe she feels travelling alone, a single woman in her thirties. For some reason I see her position as more vulnerable than my own, probably because she is pretty and therefore more likely to attract male admirers, something not likely to happen to me. I laugh to myself; she'd be faster at running away though should the need arise. However, her situation makes me realise how some people I've met on this trip might view me.

The time soon passes, most of the passengers take the opportunity to have a snooze, I on the other hand wile away the time reading, a crime fiction by Angela Marsons. We arrive twenty minutes ahead of schedule and are immediately directed to Immigration. So far on this trip, I've entered a new country by air, car, on foot and now by boat and, unlike my first solo trip to South America, I've become rather blasé at moving from one country to another, Consequently, I'm confused just for a moment, I've forgotten I'm in a different country.

Having gone through passport control, I wait outside for my driver, but yet again there is no-one to meet me off the boat. The other passengers soon disperse, and I'm left alone, although this time it is mid afternoon and therefore still light. A narrow road stretches in front of me with the water either side and at the end there is another wider road traversing it. Should I walk down and see if I can get a cab to my hotel? My problem is I have no idea if my accommodation is in the vicinity or a couple of hours drive away. I have the hotel address on me and see it is in Laguna Bacalar and not where I am in Chetumal. So, I wait it out, still undecided what to do.

Eventually, a car door opens about fifty metres away and a man gets out. He casually leans against the car, finishing his cigarette, then takes his time to amble towards me. It's my driver; I guess in theory he is on time because my boat was early, but he would have been able to see it arriving from where he was sitting and therefore must have known I'd be waiting. I'm not best pleased, my hanging around had only been for twenty minutes or so but when you don't know what's happening, the situation can be worrying. And after the lack of transport to meet me when I arrived at San Pedro, I feared this would be a similar incident.

The driver receives a stony look from me when we reach my hotel forty minutes later, but he seems oblivious; he's quickly on his way again, no doubt to meet passengers off the next boat. Needless to say, I don't give him a tip.

The lake is one of the largest in Mexico but much to my disappointment, there is no walking route skirting it from where I'm staying. Shame, I would have liked to take a stroll along the banks of the beautiful Laguna Bacalar.

I notice a pontoon and see people jumping off it into the water, and think a swim would be nice, but it's very crowded and too frenetic for my liking. Instead, I take a few photos and then make a beeline for the restaurant on the lake shore to decide whether it would be a good place to eat tonight. Having looked at the menu, I return to my hotel and read through the remainder of my itinerary; it doesn't seem possible I'm on the last leg with only a few days left.

There are a few stragglers from their day at the lake in the restaurant when I return, and a couple of tourists like me, but otherwise it is quiet. My list of cocktails has grown during my trip, however there is one which I wanted to save until Mexico, a Margarita. I've had the drink before on a few trips to stay with a friend in Arizona, but it's the one I mostly associate with Mexico. When it arrives, the cocktail tastes as good as I remember and brings back memories of my time staying in Mesa; the Amerindian culture, the flea market there, the old mining town of Goldfield, desert walks as soon as dawn awakens in order to beat the heat, and above all else, the great company. Amazing how one taste of a drink, and I guess it would be the same for food, can have that effect.

A woman comes over to speak to me. 'Hello, welcome, are you here on holiday? I am the wife of the owner, we have a Mariachi band later tonight, I hope you'll stay for it.' Sounds interesting, I've heard of the style of music before but never seen it played live. I munch on the nachos I've ordered, served with a generous amount of beef, refried beans, smashed avocado, sour cream, grated cheese and small rings of jalapenos dotted about, sip my drink and watch the lake gradually coming to stillness at the end of the day.

A few people are gathering in one area of the bar, peering out over the lake, and pointing to something in the distance. My curiosity is satisfied when the owner's wife comes over again and says, 'They are looking at the yellow moon, have you ever seen one?'

No, I hadn't, so I go over and join them. The huge round spectacle is just as she told me, yellow, an unusual sight for me. I've heard of red moons and blue ones, but never this colour. It hovers over the water, slowly spreading a pool of light over the surface, the reflection getting larger and larger before it eventually sinks and disappears, providing me with another unexpected image from this trip.

I return to my seat, and the waiter brings me a second margarita, which I hadn't ordered. 'Compliments of the house,' he says looking over to the owner's wife. She smiles, nods her head. I raise my glass in return; what a nice gesture!

The Mariachi band has arrived by now and its seven members are setting up. The restaurant is filling up and there is a frisson of excitement in anticipation of the music starting. The musicians are all dressed in brightly coloured folk costumes, the women in off the shoulder dresses and the men in flamboyantly decorated jackets and trousers, with wide brimmed hats. If you remember The Cisco Kid on TV, you'll know what I mean. Was his sidekick called Pancho? Anyway, dressed like him.

The music starts up, the combination of guitars, violins and brass instruments combining to create a lively sound. Everybody is soon into the spirit of the evening, and couples are dancing already. I sit and watch and tap my feet along with the rhythm. Funny how the least expected happening can give one so much pleasure.

The next day, I'm sitting on the veranda of the hotel waiting for my car to collect me. I wait and wait and wait some more. Not again, I contemplate, this will be the third time someone has failed to pick me up at the arranged time. I take a few long deep breaths, trying to calm down the irritation building inside me, and remember the talking to I gave myself before setting off on this trip about accepting things might not always go to plan, but after forty-five minutes, it's becoming increasingly difficult. The hotel receptionist comes over with a message to say the driver and guide had gotten lost but would be with me in another fifteen minutes!

'Janis, Janis Coley,' I hear a voice call from the street below. I look over the rail and down to where the voice is coming from. I see someone, childlike in stature; he is wearing a black waistcoat and trousers with a brilliant white shirt, on his head is a Panama hat, and he is leaning on a walking stick. He calls out again, 'Janis Coley, are you up there?'

'Yes,' I reply, annoyingly. I don't like the fact that my name is being shouted out. Another man comes rushing up behind him, the driver I later find out, and starts to climb the stairs up to the hotel.

'Lo siento,' he says breathlessly, and bows. By this time, I'm in no mood for apologies and shake my head. We are soon seated in the car; there is a third man in the passenger seat which means I share the back seat with this tiny man who had been calling out my name. He introduces himself as Manuel, the guide, and tells me the driver's name is Daniel, he also explains the other person is also a driver and apologises for their tardiness. I'm not happy and shoo away his apologies, the deep breathing hasn't helped and I'm still feeling pretty p****d off. We drive in silence for some time before we eventually stop at a small town and the passenger in the front gets out. Manual explains, 'He did the driving coming and he is going home now, he lives here. Do you want to stop for a toilet break? We will make anther stop in an hour if not.'

I shake my head. 'No thank you, how long is the journey to Merida then?' I ask.

Manuel replies, 'Four and a half to five hours, which is why we had two drivers. I'm sorry for the delay in collecting you, we left at seven thirty this morning, but the tour company gave us the wrong address in Bacalar, that is the reason we were delayed.'

I'm beginning to feel remorseful about my off-handedness, they've been journeying since early morning and must be equally fed up with the situation. 'I apologise for my manner,' I say, and then explain how things haven't gone to plan since I arrived in Mexico, and also on my arrival in Belize.

We stop at a roadside service station; I'm not hungry but notice a juice bar. While Manuel and Daniel purchase something to eat, (by now they've spent nine hours of the day travelling in the car), I join the short queue to buy a drink. There are two women in front of me who can't seem to make up their mind what to order. I must agree, the choice is comprehensive, but they seem unaware there are by now other people also waiting. They eventually order and the server, only one of them, starts to prepare their drink. I look over to Manuel and Daniel who have nearly finished eating by now. I catch Daniel's eye, tap my watch, and shrug my shoulders, as if to ask whether I have enough time? He comes dashing over. 'No hay problema,' he says. And then in broken English, 'You take time.' He gives me the broadest of smiles and returns to finish eating. I feel even more guilty about the way I reacted to them being late to collect me. He really is proving to be a sweetie.

Manuel takes a phone call from his office and from what I can make out, he is explaining how dissatisfied I was when they arrived late to pick me up. At the end of the call, he announces, to make up for the delay, the company would like to buy me a meal of my choice when we eventually get to Merida. I feel I should be begging forgiveness; their kindness is overwhelming.

It is dark when we finally reach the city, and my companions have been on the road for twelve hours. They take me to a restaurant offering Yucatan cooking and I ask them for a recommendation. There is much discussion between us, type of cuisine, vegetarian or not, chicken, beef, or pork, spicy? In the end they choose pollo pebil for me. I'm as hungry as a horse and am salivating while we sit and wait in the restaurant for my takeaway meal to be prepared.

My hotel looks a delight when we arrive; although it is nighttime, I can still see the brightly painted blue walls, wrought iron gates and big dark wooden doors. I'm guessing it was a private residence once and has now been converted into a hotel. My room is across a courtyard and several metres away from the one next door. I don't bother doing anything else other than sitting down and opening my food parcel from the restaurant; it is presented wrapped in a banana leaf and is chicken marinated in orange and achiote seeds then cooked in the oven. Black bean puree and pickled cabbage accompany the dish. It's a little on the greasy side but I devour the whole lot anyway.

The luxury of having an uninterrupted four nights in one hotel is appealing, I quickly unpack before tiredness takes over. I've done nothing today except sit in a car but am looking forward to my bed.

I sleep well and feel ready for my new adventure when I wake up the next morning. I like my room; it is spacious and tastefully decorated in a modern Hispanic style and includes a comfy sitting area. While I'm brushing my teeth, I think how perfectly the countertop basin would go in my wet room at home; it is an irregular round shape in a grey and sand coloured ceramic. Do you think they'd notice if it went missing, could I possibly smuggle it in my luggage?

Daniel is there to greet me outside the hotel; he is still smiling despite the marathon journey yesterday. Manuel is perched on a low wall, this time sporting a bright orange kerchief to accompany his attire; he reminds me of a Mexican version of Yoda from Star Wars with his small stature, weathered face and twinkling eyes. As we drive, I discover he has a sharp sense of humour as well, and both he and Daniel make for good company. 'Do you speak French?' Manuel asks me, 'Or Spanish?' I explain I'd studied French at school and also have a smattering of Spanish, more vocabulary than sentence construction though. And so, our conversations develop with the odd French sentence thrown in or me making an attempt to include Daniel by asking a question in Spanish.

Our journey passes quickly and before I realise it, we've arrived at our destination, Uxmal, the first of two ancient Mayan sites I'll be visiting in Mexico and considered to be one of the most important sites of Mayan culture.

It feels different from Tical in Costa Rica, there isn't as much shade for a start, there is also has a greater variety of construction, and the stone is more decorative. We climb roughly hewn shallow steps, and I'm worried about Manuel's ability to navigate them, but with the help of his walking stick he manages and is actually less out of breath than me when we reach the large open plaza. Here we sit and, with Manuel's excellent commentary, I get a more of an insight into Uxmal's significance for the Mayan people. I look around me as he talks and marvel at the detail in the recesses and on the corners of walls which still exist after thousands of years.

I can see something moving out of the corner of my eye but when I turn my head, nothing is there. Maybe a bird, I think. The only other people in this part of the site with us are a woman with two children and they are nowhere nearby. Again, something moves to my right, about fifteen metres away and a couple of metres above my eyeline. I look again and see a stone platform, but there's no sign of a bird. Maybe it was a leaf, I think, although the breeze is non-existent. This time, I keep my focus there and wait for any signs of movement, then, all of a sudden, I notice it, an iguana, its mottled skin a perfect match to the grey and beige shades of its surroundings. I've seen one or two already in Costa Rica, but this one is much closer. The camouflage is so extraordinarily clever that blink and you could miss it. I'm fascinated by being able to see the creature up close, and also by the way it's body uncannily melds into the background.

When we climb down and move on to another area, I see another on the ground, this one smaller; again, its colour, now slightly lighter, makes it difficult to spot at first glance. I'm even closer to this one, only a few metres away, and I can see the detail in the skin more clearly. I take a quick video clip, marvelling at how the iguana can subtly change colour to suit the environment.

Next, we visit the ball court, an area used to play the Mayan ball game. Evidently the ball was made of rubber strands to make a hard solid mass, making the most of the rubber trees which grew in abundance in Central America, and the aim was to score a goal by launching it through a stone circle high up on the side walls. My granddaughter has been watching a TV programme about the Mayans and knows about the ball game, she wants me to take a photo of the 'goal' to send back to her, which I dutifully do. How come I've never heard of the game before, but she has, just like the quetzal bird?

Manuel explains the contest was sometimes used to decide conflict between Mayan communities; they would send a team to play against each other, rather than going to war. At the end of the game, one of the winning team, (yes, the winners) was sacrificed. I asked, 'Why would they try to win then?' Evidently, if you are sacrificed, their belief was you could be reincarnated in one year. Otherwise, it would take four years, in order to judge if you were worthy enough.

I've enjoyed my visit to Uxmal with its well-preserved stone carvings of animals' heads and ancient Mayan symbols. Here, it's been possible to immerse myself more because I've been able to climb amongst some of the ruins, unlike Tical in that respect, although the latter's setting in the jungle made it visually more appealing.

We get back to my accommodation in the late afternoon, and I have the chance to enjoy my hotel for the rest of the day. It was, as I suspect, a private residence originally and dates from the sixteenth century. Many of the original features are still present; vaulted ceilings with wooden beams, decorative ironwork, and tall wooden doors, also the house was designed with three inner courtyards, I'm guessing to help with airflow in the hot climate. Some of the communal rooms have been given a modern twist with funky artwork; a wooden mobile hangs from the ceiling in one corner, a huge acrylic painting of two native hunters is displayed on a wall in the bar. The long lounge however retains the traditionality. One side is made of glass like a conservatory and looks out on a pretty courtyard, although I suspect it was originally open to the elements. Long bookshelves and display cabinets occupy another side; there are paintings on another while the fourth one leads into the dining room. Large potted plants, standard lamps, vases, and comfy sofas fill the room. I sit down in an armchair and order a pina colada, my fifteenth different cocktail of the trip. I could easily lose a couple of hours in here if I fancied a change from my room.

We had stopped for lunch on our way back from Uxmal, consequently I decide I won't want any dinner this evening. Instead, I stroll back to my room later and go to bed early.

The next day I'm on a city tour to visit the main sights; an old church, the main square, spoilt in my opinion by the sign MERIDA in assorted colours, stuck in the middle. I have the obligatory photo taken in front of it, just as I did in Panama, Lima, and Montevideo, and then we're back in the car and off to look at something else. Manuel asks me, 'Some people don't like to visit cemeteries, but would you like me to show you the main one in Merida?' I readily agree; I know from experience these places can reveal much about a culture.

We wander around the graveyard, looking at vaults and headstones, while Manuel talks about the resting places of the various people to have played a significant role in the history of the Yucatan peninsular. His words don't really engage me; I can feel my attention after five weeks of absorbing information has waned, but what does interest me are the colours of some of the headstones. A bright magenta one catches my eye, then another, equally colourful in jade. They vary in construction, and I find it bizarre to see them in a graveyard. We come across a terracotta one. 'Why are some of them brightly coloured?' I ask. 'Do the colours have a particular significance?'

'Sometimes the families paint them in the favourite colour of the person who has died,' Manuel explains. 'You'll find them throughout Central America but mostly in Mexico. Do you like the idea?' They certainly add another dimension to the otherwise sombre environment.

I'm not ready to return to my hotel yet and ask to be dropped off in the city centre when we've finished the tour. Today is the second to last day of my trip and I want to make the most of it. A friend had sent me a link to an article about Merida and in it is mentioned a particular gelato shop. I noticed it when we visited the main square earlier, just around the corner from where I've been left. I turn off into a side street and there is the shop sitting in a small square next to a hotel. The choices, when I go inside, all sound tempting, making selection difficult, but in the end, I settle on a scoop of peach and another of salted caramel. Yes, I'm definitely a two-scoop kind of person. I sit on a bench outside in the shade and soak up the atmosphere; visitors come in and out of the hotel, a few locals wander into the church, and the odd tourist takes photos of a statue across the street. I would like to tell you I'm taking my time to enjoy the ice cream, but it's a well-known fact for my nearest and dearest that I always devour my ice creams quicker than you can say gelato! Nevertheless, I still sit and watch the world go by about me for some time after the last crumb of cone has passed my lips.

I take the chance to browse the shops, although most of my buying has already been completed. Do I need another Panama hat, I ponder, looking in a shop window? The price is more expensive than the ones I bought in Panama, and none bear the name Montecristi, so I desist. I do however buy T-shirts for the grandchildren, bright orange, blue and red ones with Merida emblazoned across the front.

I exit the shop and look up and down the street, now which way is back to the hotel? I thought I knew the route but now I'm not sure which direction to go in. The streets are laid out in a grid system; this is the fifty ninth and I know the hotel is in the fifty seventh, a mere two blocks away, but in the afternoon heat I don't want to make more walking for myself than is necessary. Which way to turn? I go back into the shop and ask the woman who has just sold me the T-shirts, however, she doesn't speak English. I make a stab at asking in Spanish and am relieved when she understands. 'Gira a la derecha y gira al la derecha de nuevo,' she tells me. I recognise the words for turn right, and with help from her gesticulations as well, I manage to find my road.

The houses in the heritage quarter where I'm staying remind me of the old parts of Antigua and Flores; the original buildings still exist, their brightly coloured painted exteriors displaying the whole spectrum of the rainbow. Despite the heat, I keep stopping to take photos of them; they look very pretty standing side by side. I cross over the street in order to walk in the shade and pass a restaurant with two life size figures sitting on a bench in the entrance; they've been dressed in Mexican folk costumes, rather like the Mariachi band I saw in Bacalar, however their faces are skulls and they remind me of the James Bond film set in New Orleans during Mardi Gras. Was it Licence to Kill or Live and Let Die? I wonder if voodoo is practised in Mexico.

I arrive back at my hotel without getting lost and decide a sit by the pool is what's called for. The water is exceptionally cold, otherwise a dip might have been on the cards. I read a little and probably doze as well. Before I know it, dinner time is upon me. Only one more day in Mexico left.

Today is a visit to Chichen Itza, the largest city in the Mayan civilisation and the only ancient Mayan site I'd heard of before coming on this trip. It is much busier than either Uxmal or Tical; the dirt road from the car park to the site is lined with stalls selling souvenirs which somehow detract from the atmosphere I'd experienced at the other sites.

This time Manuel leaves me by the Kukulkan Temple, allowing me to wander at my leisure. I walk round the grand looking stepped pyramid, the image one is likely to see in photos, and I notice how different it is from the main one at Uxmal, the Temple of the Magicians, although both are magnificent. Although these buildings were often painted red, as were other Mayan temples and palaces, some were also painted blue and green. It must have been quite a sight.

There is another ball court here; the stone rings through which the ball had to pass in order to score, are even higher than at Uxmal, about six metres off the ground I would think. I marvel at the thought of the players propelling the ball when the rules stated they weren't allowed to touch it with their hands, only their torsos and heads. Evidently, the game could go on for several days.

Each of the sites I've visited has had something different to offer, Chichen Itza being the best preserved one, however I enjoyed Tical and Uxmal more. There was no opportunity to clamber among the ruins today and the crowds of people here made it more like a spectacle than an experience.

I've been out in the sun for a good few hours today and I'm weary by the time we return to the car. On the way back, Manuel starts to say something to me. Daniel puts his finger to his lips; he has noticed in his rearview mirror my eyes are closed and I'm taking a rest. It is those odd moments of kindness and awareness of my needs which I like about the two of them. I shall miss this pair when it's time to say goodbye.

My well-deserved shower after a dusty and sweltering day was refreshing and I'm now sitting in the lounge looking at a photo book of the area and waiting for my last evening meal of my trip to be prepared. Another margarita sits in front of me; the saltiness around the rim accompanying the sharpness of the lime and the kick of the tequila and triple sec make for pleasant tasting. A fellow guest comes into the lounge, someone I'd exchanged pleasantries with the evening before. Her name is Jan too and she is staying here with her granddaughter.

'May I talk to you about your trip?' She enquires. 'My husband and I used to do a lot of travelling but he passed away last year, and I've been hesitant about going on trips like you're doing by myself.' We talk for a while about my experience as a solo traveller, the possible hurdles as well as the wonderful opportunities that can create themselves.

My dinner is ready and as I stand to go into the dining room, Jan says, 'Talking to you has given me the confidence to try solo travel. You're an inspiration, thank you.' Her comment fills me with joy; I'm delighted if I can help give someone the incentive to go it alone.

The next morning, I pack away my wash bag, zip up my case, check my passport, credit cards and what currency I have left are all safely in my bum bag, and sit down to wait for a call from reception to say my car to take me to the airport is here. How the time has flown, but I feel ready now to end my trip. I've visited five countries in total, stayed in ten different accommodations, taken five internal flights, six boat trips and travelled I don't know how many miles by car. And the number of cocktails I've tried hasn't been too shabby either. Much as I've enjoyed this adventure, five weeks is a long time to be away, and I'll be glad to get home and return to familiarity. At least, that is, until the next trip!

The trip was undertaken in 2024

Weeks later, on my return, I talk to my daughter's partner about the conversation I'd had with Jan, and he suggests I should write a blog about my travels, called Seventy-Five Feeling Alive. Instead, I decide to draft a book, this book. So, Jan, should you by chance ever read this, thank you for your kind comment and for actually being my inspiration.

Temple of the Magicians - Uxmal

Cemetery at Merida

Daniel and Manuel, my driver and guide

Chichen Itza, best preserved Mayan site in Mexico

An Aside - I'm Not a Cocktail Girl

Having a cocktail used to sound so glamorous, conjuring up images of chic black dresses, long, satin gloves, an ermine stole draped nonchalantly round the shoulders, sitting in the American bar at the Savoy with one knee elegantly wrapped across the other, cigarette holder in one hand and conical Martini glass in the other. For some reason, the attraction seemed to go out of fashion for several years, only to reinvent itself in the 2000s, except the trend on its revival now appealed to a wider range of clientele, not only the rich and famous. The cocktail has become a popular tipple on a night out, a treat, a moment of spoilaciousness.

Over time, different spirits have come to the fore and into fashion, also exotic fruit juices. A wider range of liqueurs have become more familiar too. While well established cocktails such as sidecar, screwball or Harvey Wallbanger are still popular, some of the newer concoctions conjure up images of places or occasions we might want to be a part of, drinks like blue lagoon, tequila sunrise, sex on the beach, or even porn Martini. In addition to the ingredients, the look may have also changed, and cocktails can now come with all sorts of toppings, things like foam and flamed meringue adding to their delight.

It was a chance conversation one Xmas when it was decided the challenge I should set myself on my tour of Central America. A family member was browsing through a cocktail book he had received as a Xmas present and came across one from Panama, a country I would be visiting on my trip. He suggested I should aim to try a typical cocktail from each of the countries on my itinerary. The task was adapted as we discussed the possibilities, and we eventually agreed I should see how many different cocktails I could try in the five weeks I was away, rather than a different one from each country.

I have to declare, cocktails wouldn't be my first choice of drink, although at one time I did own a classy looking silver cocktail shaker, picked up at a car boot sale, but never actually used it. And I have enjoyed the odd cocktail in the past; I can recall having a peach bellini made by my nephew as an accompaniment to a family Boxing Day brunch. The combination of sparkling wine and peach juice went down well and was a change, providing a fantastic way to refresh the palate after the overload of flavours on my tastebuds from Christmas Day.

Other cocktails I've tried have shocked my gustatory sense, like the vodka Martini I was served on a transatlantic flight once. I had no idea beforehand of the proportions and expected the taste to be like a vermouth with a bit of a kick. One generous sip and it hit me. I hadn't realised that in fact the measurements are three or four times the amount of vodka to vermouth. It would be an understatement to say the explosion of vodka on my palate took me by surprise.

I'm not much of a spirits person anyway, the occasionally JD and coke or a nip of brandy in my cappuccino over the Xmas period is enough for me, although I did enjoy the pisco sours I drank on my South American trip. However, I came to the conclusion, I actually preferred the pisco by itself.

But what of the cocktail challenge on my Central American trip? In all I tried fifteen different concoctions during my five weeks away, from daiquiris to pina coladas then mojitos through to bar specialities, but for the most part I found them underwhelming. And as for Happy Hour!! It seemed to be an excuse to apportion the same measure of alcohol between two glasses then fill to the top with whatever non alcoholic mixer was supposed to be present in the drink.

Talking of different cocktails, the most unusual one I've ever set eyes on was during a food tour in New Orleans. 'Is this the place you can get a pickled vodka Bloody Mary?' Enquired one of the group when we sat down in a bar for our po'boys tasting. The drink, I was told when it had been tried, tasted like pickle juice. It was adorned with slices of crispy bacon and haricots vert, to use as stirrers I guess, and a wedge of lemon. The most peculiar looking cocktail I've ever come across.

I'm always fascinated watching the cocktail expert, Merlin Griffiths on James Martin's Saturday Morning TV programme. Is that his real name and coincidental he shares it with the character from Arthurian legend? Both it would seem have made alchemy their business. The mixtures he comes up with are fascinating, both alcoholic and non alcoholic, and his flamboyancy in preparing and pouring the drink is a work of art in itself. His selections sound so tempting.

    Which cocktails have I found to tickle my fancy then? One I enjoyed while I was in New Orleans was bourbon with maraschino cherry liqueur and sweet vermouth, served in a small wine glass with neither a straw nor ice in sight. I remember savouring the sweetness of the vermouth and cherry on my taste buds combined with the heat of the spirits as I sipped.

Beware enjoying a cocktail too much though. A few years ago, I was invited to a reading of Charles Dickens The Hours in the same building, now a barrister's chambers in Gray's Inn, where the author first read his story to a group of esteemed friends. There was an assortment of drinks for the guests to enjoy both before and after the reading including one, I was reliably informed, called rum sneeze, (mentioned by Dickens in his writings and discovered by him on his reading tour of America). I can't exactly remember all the ingredients or measurements other than it contained rum, brandy, sugar and not much else. The drink was exceptionally strong but so tasty that a second one seemed to fit in with the conviviality of the evening, (and it was just a couple of weeks before Xmas). Not a wise idea. The trouble is if you find a cocktail you like, then they're very moreish and it's easy to give in to temptation. However, I learnt how unwise it is to get too carried away. Thank goodness I didn't try rum sneeze till later in the evening, otherwise I would have been non compos mentis for the reading. As it was, I couldn't recall much about my journey home on the tube that evening.

It must sound like, for someone who declares she's not a cocktail girl, I've listed an awful lot of tried cocktails. But I guess, over the nearly sixty years of being legally old enough to buy alcohol, my consumption would average only one every two or three years, and that statistic includes all those I tried in Central America.

So, there you have it, a brief account of my cocktail experiences. But you know, if the truth be told, I'm a simple girl at heart. When push comes to shove, you can keep them, I'd prefer a glass of wine any day.

Pickled vodka Bloody Mary

UNITED STATES OF AMERICA

Southern Sights and Sounds

I've prattled on about long solo trips in other chapters and how good they can be, but travel doesn't have to be totally by oneself or for an extended period of time to be fun, and if you're not ready to go away completely on your own, then an escorted tour might suit you just as well. Last year I took myself off on one to the United States, a group tour visiting four southern states: Georgia, Tennessee, Louisiana and Alabama, and including Memphis, Nashville, and New Orleans, three cities with mega music connections.

My impressions of escorted tours I've taken in the past is that they are generally patronised by two people travelling together. I wondered what the experience would be like for me then as a solo traveller; the previous times I'd been on escorted tours was when I had travelled with a friend.

The trip ticked a number of boxes on my wish list, consequently it was the itinerary which persuaded me. The thought of visits to Studio B, Gracelands and the Grand Ole Opry was enticing. The itinerary also included Montgomery, Atlanta, and Monroeville, where there would be opportunities to improve my knowledge of the Civil Rights movement in the US.

I wondered whether I'd be viewed as a Billy No Mates by my fellow travellers, someone who everybody is polite to but wary of too much interaction with, for fear of being lumbered, like a limpet which can't be shaken off. Or perhaps someone to feel sorry for, not being able to find anyone to accompany them on the trip. I expect these thoughts have gone through some people's minds when trying to decide whether to embark on this type of holiday alone. However, any doubts I had proved to be unfounded, and it turned out to be one of the best holidays I've ever been on. Certainly, the best escorted tour.

We arrive at our hotel in Atlanta; as with most escorted tours, porterage is included, consequently I can choose whether I wait until my case has been delivered to my room or save time by taking it myself. I choose the latter, thank goodness for the invention of wheelie cases. A quick unpack of the essentials as we're only here for one night, and then bed. We have been advised not to wander around the area outside by ourselves at night, this isn't something I'm fussed about, what I need at the moment is sleep.

 The next morning, I go in search of breakfast and have a recce of the hotel to see what's on offer. I've mentioned in previous chapters how I like to start the day with a good breakfast while I'm away, it means I don't have to worry about lunch then, usually taking a pastry and piece of fruit from breakfast to have later. There is a wide selection in the restaurant buffet and only a few other early risers to share it with, mostly businesspeople I would think from their appearance. I find a table and check out the itinerary for the day while I enjoy my breakfast choices.

 My case has been already collected from outside my room and taken to be put on the coach by the time I make my way down to the lobby for the first full day of the tour. There is a seat plan already waiting for us on the coach and I look to see where I'll be sitting. I find the seat rotation policy generally adopted by travel companies is a good way of connecting with others in the group, it means you're sitting across the aisle from different people each day; a good morning or smile and a nod to a fresh face creates opportunities for you to get to know your fellow travellers better. You don't have to engage in chat but the option to share your thoughts is there. And of course, the rotation policy gives everyone a chance to be near the front of the coach some of the time.

We learn many facts about Atlanta as we start our tour of the city; did you know there are over seventy streets here with Peachtree in their name, which must be confusing for visitors. The headquarters of Coca Cola, American Express and CNN are here but, interestingly, despite being a mega business metropolis, we see few pedestrians. We're told this is because a network of aerial walkways has been built to link the office buildings; it seems strange not to see more people out on the streets.

Our guide tells us about the author Margaret Mitchell as we pass her house. Gone with The Wind, a love story set against the backdrop of the American Civil War, won her a Pulitzer Prize, but how she came about writing it is intriguing. When she broke her ankle, her husband bought her a typewriter to keep her occupied during convalescence and the result was the much-lauded historical novel. Funny how things sometimes work out, isn't it? What's even more bizarre is that she penned the first chapter of the book last and the last chapter first.

A visit to the Martin Luther King National Park gives us our first insight about the background of the Civil Rights movement. A statue of Kunta Kinte, from Alex Haley's book Roots, stands at the entrance, reminding me of the powerfully moving TV drama series and the book on which it was based. I spend some time in the museum there, also in Ebenezer Baptist Church where both King and his father used to preach. A church warden is giving a free talk; he talks animatedly and with pride about the church and its legacy.

After lunch, we leave Atlanta to move onto our next stop; it has been a whirlwind of a morning, and I can understand why a few of the tour group chose to come out a day earlier than the rest of us. There is certainly plenty to see in this city.

We cross the state line into Tennessee and say hello to the cardboard cut out life sized figure of Dolly Parton in the visitors' centre. There are a number of leaflets available, advertising different things to see and do across the state, and my fellow group members take advantage of them before continuing the journey to Chattanooga.

After checking in, I take a walk to seek out somewhere to eat. 'Come and have a drink,' I hear a voice call out. It is one of the other solo travellers on my trip sitting with a few of our group. I cross the street and join them. We end up going to dinner together except now we are a group of nine.

On my pre-breakfast walk the next day I have the chance to get a better idea of Chattanooga. Wall and shop signs always fascinate me and there are plenty on display here. An advertisement for moon pies, (I've never heard of the name before), reminds me of what I remember as wagon wheels; I wonder if they're the same. Haven't seen them for a long time at home though, do they still sell them in England? I also notice a sign above a shop saying Pinball Museum; it's not open yet, otherwise I would have gone in, but it's the first one I've come across. There's another sign emblazoned in large letters on a side wall overlooking a parking lot, announcing, 'Change Starts in Your Own Backyard.' I'm not sure what it's advertising but how true.

Our first visit today is to the Jack Daniel's distillery in Lynchburg to discover what gives the bourbon its distinctive taste. I learn that the slave who first worked for Jack Daniels actually taught him the distilling techniques which continue to be used to this day. He had the very unusual name of Nearest Green and at least one member of his family has always worked for the company. Yes, even now! I do like a bit of provenance.

We're told water from the natural spring is one key ingredient, also that the distilling process uses a hardwood charcoal called Sugar Maple for filtering. This charcoal pulls out some of the impurities, thus adding to the smoothness of the whiskey's flavour. At the end of the tour, we have the chance to try six varieties of Jack Daniels. What a fantastic way to finish the morning.

Chattanooga Station is like stepping back into a bygone era. The rails are only used for transporting freight now, but the line once played a strategic part in the American Civil War, because of the town's geographic position. I take photos of the Chattanooga Choo Choo, the train which inspired a song, and then have a wander around the huge, now unused, original ticket hall with its high decorative ceiling. I try to conjure up a picture in my mind of what it would have been like during the golden era of rail travel in the early twentieth century. I can almost see and hear the hustle and bustle; cabs drawing up outside to unload their passengers, honking their horns, porters busily scurrying about to unload luggage and transport it to the waiting train, children with their parents chatting excitedly about the trip, and businessmen looking up at the giant clock to check the time or glancing through their newspapers while they puff on their cigarettes.

With the rest of the afternoon free, I decide to visit the Hunter Museum; you often get another perspective of a place from an art gallery. The relatively small exhibition makes it easy to browse; a picture grabs my attention, the collage by Bisa Butler is made using fabric and depicts a negro family dressed in their Sunday best. It reminds me of the Yinka Shonibare works I'd seen at the Serpentine Gallery a few months earlier.

We move on to Nashville the next day and our guide has offered to take to us a restaurant, the Nashville Palace, with live music. The country and western band is already playing when we arrive, a number of locals are up on their feet, showing their moves; some couples dance the two step while others are line dancing. How can I resist the temptation to get up and join in when the music is so inviting? I love the saying 'Dance like no-one is watching………' And I do. The chances are I would never meet these people again, so does it matter what they might think of me? So, between bites of ribs and glugs of beer, I dance the night away, sometimes joining in with the sequences and at other times doing my own thing. Some members of my group are on their feet too and the line dancers are more than willing to help us master the steps and constant changes of direction required; their patience is much appreciated. It's unimportant whether we can keep up with the well-practised regulars, (although at least two of our group are seasoned line dancers, I find out. They've even brought their cowboy boots with them.) What a fab evening.

Our first 'music stop' the next day is to the hallowed recording venue, Studio B, where artists such as Elvis Presley, The Everly Brothers, Jim Reeves, Brenda Lee, Dolly Parton, and many other big names recorded. The visit brings back all sorts of memories for me as a teenager in the sixties. To sit in the actual recording studio and hear the various stories about those mega stars gives me goosebumps, and to stand on the exact spot where the artists would have stood when they were making the recording is amazing. I could almost feel their presence. It was fascinating as well to hear anecdotes about some of the stars. Did you know that when Elvis Presley recorded his Xmas albums, months before the festive season, he would have the studio filled with Xmas decorations to help create the right mood?

Another story we hear about is the recording of *Are You Lonesome Tonight*. Presley didn't want to record it but agreed to as long as he only had to do one take. All the lights in the recording area were turned off, again to create the right mood, he did the one take and that was it, except for one slight problem. The sound technician had turned off the machine slightly too early, and that's why, if you listen carefully, you can hear a click at the end of the recording.

We also learn how Presley wanted to record Dolly Parton's *I Will Always Love You*, but he insisted he should be paid the royalties, rather than the normal practice of the songwriter receiving them. Parton refused him, a bold decision given his status and selling power at the time. The song was subsequently used in the film *The Bodyguard*, sung by Whitney Houston; Parton concluded the royalties from that one song would have been enough for her to buy Gracelands, Presley's home, so big a hit did it become.

The coach drops us off round the corner from a four-storey building in the centre of Nashville, on the corner of Broadway. The Country Hall of Fame is dedicated to every country and western musician you're likely to have heard of. Interesting to wander around inside but not enough to engage me for long. It is the hub of activity outside which I'm drawn to. Broadway is a street that is home to forty bars, each one with a live band playing country music. You don't even need to venture inside them if you choose not to, many have the musicians playing next to wide open windows where you can peep in or just stand outside and listen. *Islands In the Stream, We're Having a Party, Take Me Home, Achy Breaky Heart*, it's like listening to a catalogue of the best country and western music ever written. Party buses go by; some are motor driven while others rely on the pedal power of their participants, while inside the bars, people wave and cheer at them then raise their glasses in mutual camaraderie. Still only mid-afternoon and the whole area is alive, it feels like one big party.

I've heard a lot about the Grand Ole Opry, the hallowed ground of country and western music and where every artist longs for the chance to stand in the golden circle and perform. It's odd to see, when we arrive this evening, the compere sitting behind a table on the corner of the stage ready to do his commercial spiel between acts as well as introducing each one, but it reminds the audience this is a radio show, the longest running in US history. The auditorium itself is huge, and seats over four thousand people. Tonight, it is heaving and as I look around, I can't see an empty seat anywhere.

We have been forewarned we mustn't take any drink or food items in with us, not even water. I curl my lip at the news; it's obviously a ploy to increase revenue, but I object to paying silly prices for something you can get from a tap. A few of our group have headed to the shop to buy water when I suddenly espy a woman carrying two large plastic beakers of what looks like water with ice in. Aha, I think! 'Excuse me, is that water?' I ask.

She smiles. 'Yes, you need to be a regular here to know where you can get it without paying.' She lets me into the secret. I duly do as the woman instructs me and then have the joy of watching the performance with a refreshing glass of ice-cold water in my hand for free. So, if you ever find yourself in Nashville and are going to the Grand Ole Opry, and don't want to pay for your water, take a right through the entrance and before you go in the auditorium itself, keep walking until you're nearly at the end. On your left you'll see an ice machine and a stack of plastic glasses. Just help yourself!

I had asked one of the ticket checkers on my way in who would be performing that evening and which artist he thought was the standout performer, and he said with a typical Tennessee drawl, 'Well darlin', for me it has to be Don Schlitz.'

I try to look interested but never having heard of him before, it was difficult. 'Why him?' I ask, rapidly trying to rack my brains for some tiny recollection of the name.

'You'll see. Have a great evening now,' was all the man would say, giving me a wink before he turned his attention to checking another group's tickets.

And he proves to be right, well for me anyway. There are six acts in all, including Carrie Underwood, a previous winner of American Pop Idol, who is headlining the show. All of them are brilliant, but I agree with the ticket checker, Mr Schlitz is the artist I enjoy the most. If the name isn't familiar to you, then it's probably because he is better known as a songwriter than a singer, but if I tell you he wrote (and sang that evening,) *You Know it Best When You Say Nothing At All,* and the iconic *The Gambler,* you may have a better understanding of his reputation in the music industry. As for the show itself, it is everything I hoped for and more. A wonderful evening!

Today we move on to Memphis but make a stop in Tupelo on the way to visit the birthplace and childhood home of Elvis Presley. The tiny two roomed house and the church where he attended Sunday services, are the perfect precursor to our visit to Gracelands the next day.

As if the dancing in Nashville hadn't been enough, it continues that evening. Many of the Memphis eateries in the famed Beale Street, also have live bands playing. Some of us opt to go to BB Kings; what can I say, the ribs are to die for and the soul and blues music sublime. Does it matter if I'm the first one on the dance floor? No, I'm soon joined by others, and do you know what? It wouldn't have mattered a jot if I wasn't. How can I not succumb to the music of Aretha Franklin and Gladys Knight and the memories it evokes of me dancing around my handbag as a teenager.

Gracelands is not what I was expecting. I'd anticipated something blingy and brash, however the house turns out to be surprisingly tasteful. Even the pool room where three hundred and fifty metres of fabric had been used to line the walls and ceiling, looks classy. The house is only a small part of the experience, there are large exhibition spaces showing different facets of Presley's lifestyle as well, including his grand collection of cars. I particularly enjoy looking at his show outfits and studying the detailed workmanship which has gone into each one. Many are recognisable from his TV appearances and also from films of the numerous residencies he did in Las Vegas.

Another space contains models of the various people who have acknowledged they were influenced by him. It reads like a who's who of the music world; Elton John, John Lennon, Keith Richard, James Brown, Dolly Parton, Michael Buble and Justin Timberlake are among them. Quite a legacy.

Back in Memphis, after our visit to Gracelands, we visit Sun Records, another iconic studio from the nineteen fifties and sixties, and where Elvis Presley, Jerry Lee Lewis, Carl

Perkins, and Johnny Cash famously happened to come across each other one time. The West End musical *Million Dollar Quartet* tells the story of this chance happening when four of the greats of pop music all met.

Talking of chance happenings, on our short journey back to our hotel I find out the men with Noel Gallagher hairstyles, like the Mods of my day, I'd seen at the airport when we were queuing to get through Immigration, were members of the Buzzcocks. No, I hadn't heard of them either but have been reliably informed they were a popular band in the seventies and eighties. Evidently, they're about to begin a tour in the States. Small world!

We stop at the Lorraine Hotel, where Martin Luther King was assassinated, and during segregation, a hotel only for black people. A red and white wreath hangs from the balcony railings where King was shot, acting as a salutary reminder of what happened here and, rather like our visit to the national park bearing his name in Atlanta, it is a moving experience. The building is now home to the National Museum for Civil Rights, helping to ensure the significant sequence of events aren't forgotten.

It's our last evening in Memphis; I would have happily returned to BB Kings, but I've opted instead to join my fellow travellers at the Blues City Café, again in Beale Street. The music this time is rock and roll with a four-piece band playing. If you've ever seen clips of Jerry Lee Lewis, then you'll know what I mean when I say the man at the piano is on fire and it doesn't take long before the joint is rocking. The band belt out *Lucille, Great Balls of Fire, Let's Have a Party*, the sort of music you couldn't just sit still and listen to. Well at least I can't. Once again, I'm up on my feet at the earliest opportunity. How can I not with all that rhythm going through me? I would estimate I'm one of the oldest in the group, but I've discovered a joe de vivre on this trip and am having the time of my life. Nobody judges, nobody gives me odd looks, and nobody is embarrassed. And I'm too busy having a fun time.

The next day we set off again on the drive to New Orleans, however, on the way, we're told contingency plans are being put in place for alternative accommodation should we not be able to reach there tonight. Hurricane Francine is due to hit the area, and it's touch and go whether we'll make it to the hotel in time. We drive along a series of bridges, traversing rivers, and at each one we come to, I notice the waterline creeping a little higher each time. The driver has the windscreen wipers full on and visibility outside is poor; I wonder how he can possibly see the road, but he keeps going.

At last, we arrive, and as I step off the coach, I feel the force of the wind on my face and the rain beginning to beat down. There is a quick dash to get inside the hotel; everyone has been asked to collect any suitcase from the hold regardless of who it belongs to, speed of getting safely indoors is of the essence. A reduced number of staff means there is no porterage for us today, many of them live outside the city and have been sent home before the hurricane really hits.

I make it safely inside and collect the key to my room, however, I haven't been there for more than fifteen minutes before the room phone rings. It's the hotel services asking if I'll need any assistance should the hotel have to be evacuated, also a warning there may be a power cut. It's a reminder of the havoc the hurricane could cause. I lay out everything I might need and then look to see if there are any WhatsApp messages from the group. Our lovely tour manager had set it up at the start of the trip. A message reads, 'Happy Hour in the bar has started early.' I head downstairs straightaway.

The conviviality is infectious, is there a better place to be holed up during a hurricane than in a bar in the company of this wonderful crowd? The wind is raging outside as we look out of the glass frontage of the hotel and trees are violently being bent with the force of it, however, inside there's a party going on. It feels like every guest from the hotel is gathered here. And it continues throughout the evening, long after Happy Hour is supposed to have finished. Another glass of wine appears in front of where I'm sitting. 'On the house,' the bar steward says. Who am I to refuse?

The next morning Hurricane Francine has passed but there are a few signs of its effects still remaining on the sidewalks when I go out of the hotel. There are sandbags in front of doorways and rubbish blown everywhere, but otherwise all is calm. I speak to someone waiting to cross the road with me.' Quite a storm last night,' I say.

He smiles, shakes his head, and looks at me benignly. 'Only a one on the scale, nothing to be concerned about. We'll have worse ones.' I guess it's just a way of life for them.

We're in New Orleans for four nights, and the itinerary is for us to decide how we spend our time. Extra excursions are available at a cost but I'm mostly going to do my own thing. I've found on other trips that a food tour is a fantastic way to explore a city, and I've booked myself on one today.

I meet up with the guide and my fellow participants, none of whom I know, and we are first taken to a bar near the river. We're ushered into a back room and given a Cajun dish to try called calas; deep fried rice balls from West Africa served on a bed of honey and sprinkled with icing sugar, and I learn the word Cajun actually originates from Nova Scotia, the

Canadian province. On we go to our next stop, passing the gold statue of Joan of Arc, resplendently mounted on a horse. I recall she was known as the Maid of Orleans, although after the city in France, not the one I'm presently in. (I don't think a trip across the Atlantic was de rigeur in the Middle Ages.)

The French market is relatively quiet when we reach there and most of the stalls are closed. The vendors had left the city the day before because of the threat of the hurricane, but we're assured they'll be back the next day. However, a few of the food stalls are still open. We try a muffaletta; pastrami and Swiss cheese with pickled veg in sesame bread. I notice a food stall advertising anything alligator to eat, rather like the lobster menu I saw in Belize, but this one is more snack (or is it snap) like.

One of the group asks about a particular cocktail, pickled vodka Bloody Mary, (described in the chapter, I'm Not a Cocktail Girl). 'Yes, you can buy it at our next stop,' our guide informs her. So, while we eat our po'boy sandwich; shrimp, tomato, lettuce, and mayo served with a peppery sauce and with a kind of bread only made in New Orleans, the woman sips on her weird looking drink. Wouldn't be my choice but obviously hers.

There has to be a Creole dish somewhere on the tour, as we're in New Orleans, and we aren't disappointed when we go to another eatery and are served gumbo with chicken, pork and rice, thickened with okra and containing the trinity of creole cooking, celery, onion, and green bell pepper. I pass on the oyster and melted cheese which follows but do enjoy a praline from the New Orleans School of Cooking, to finish off the tour. Speaking of oysters, some restaurants here advertise happy hour but for oysters at one dollar a pop; somewhat cheaper than the food hall in Selfridges. It has been an excellent tour and the sort of one I would recommend in any country.

This evening I'm going on an optional excursion, a sunset dinner cruise on a paddle steamer along the Mississippi. Most of the group have chosen to go as well and we are a jolly lot as we join the many other tourists to step onboard.

The meal which is included isn't anything to write home about and the views of the river underwhelming but, hey, guess what, there is a jazz band. And you can probably work out how my evening ends up. Yes, dancing. Again!

I decide not to do the optional excursion of a city tour the next day but instead book myself on a hop on hop off bus tour. That way, if I see somewhere I want to spend more time, I can do so. The guide on board keeps up a running commentary about the various sights as we pass them and people get on and off at stops on the way. I decide to alight at Louis Armstrong Park and take a walk around. It is peaceful and relatively uncrowded with trees galore to provide shade in the thirty something degree heat. I do love a good sculpture and there a number of them here to admire, including one of Satchmo himself. The green space also houses the Mahalia Jackson Theatre for Performing Arts. How lovely to come across a park with such a strong arts focus.

I get back on the bus and take a long glug of my water; it certainly is hot today. In another few stops, the bus comes to an interesting looking street, and I decide to get off and take a wander around. 'How far is the next bus stop?' I ask the driver, thinking I could walk to it instead of waiting for the hop on hop off when I've finished here.

'If yah wants to,' she says in her southern drawl, 'you can go down here ma'am and cut off the block to get to the next stop,' she says pointing to a street to my right.

I get off the bus and take a look around. A kitchenware shop catches my eye, Ladle and the Whisk it's called, another says Gator Museum. I notice one with a row of kites on display outside, each one has a spooky face on. The breeze moves them sprightly from side to side, making them look even more ghostlike. It will be Halloween in a few weeks, and I've already noticed the shops are full of goods to buy.

I turn down a side street and come across a mural occupying up the whole of the side of a building. It says in large bold script 'Greetings from NOLA,' and it takes me a while to work out the letters stand for New Orleans Louisiana. There is a row of small colourful houses, limes and purples and hot pinks, with contrasting window frames and doors. Wooden stairs lead up to porches with swinging benches or rocking chairs. The whole area is charming, and it is a part of New Orleans I would never have come across but for the hop on hop off bus. It somehow sums up the eclectic nature of the city, artiness and commerce, poverty and wealth, African and colonial influence.

When I'm ready to move on, I turn right as instructed by the bus driver into a tree lined street and pass large houses with plaques outside saying who would have been the occupants, the likes of ships' captains, cotton merchants, and slave traders. I shake my head in despair, imagining how those people accumulated their wealth. I turn right again into a wide avenue and as I walk, I notice fragments of brightly coloured paper and fabric blowing in the breeze. The street sign says St Charles Avenue, one of the streets on the main route for the parades during Mardi Gras. These remnants of the carnival are still hanging from the overhead streetcar cables eight months after the event.

Tiredness is setting in by the time I reach the end of the road, and the bus stop is still nowhere in sight. In front of me is a slip road leading to a highway and there is another traversing my route. I look at the map but can't fathom which direction to go in. It's early afternoon, the temperature has shot up, and I've been on my feet for two hours by now, plus the time spent in the park. Thank goodness I'm wearing my wide brimmed hat and have water with me.

I take the road directly ahead and hope it's the right one. It leads me into a more built-up area and eventually I can see tall white buildings in the distance, including one with SHERATON in large letters across its front. Phew, what a relief!

Tonight, is our last night here and I still haven't visited Bourbon Street, the hub of the social scene in the city and where everyone goes for a night out. Again, there is live music in the many bars but here it's on every corner as well; a saxophonist is playing *Can't Take My Eyes Off You*, a four-piece band belts out *When the Saints Go Marching In*, and everyone is smiling. The music is infectious. A group of us sit and chat about our various experiences that day and then, after a couple of drinks, we walk back to our hotel. My intention is to go to my room and finish packing but a DJ is playing in the bar on our return and so I go and dance. Before long there is a group of us on our feet. Why spoil the trend that has been set on this trip from the very beginning?

The next day we enter another US state, Alabama, and learn more about the Deep South as we go. We stop on our journey at Monroeville and visit the courthouse. Harper Lee's father practised law here and the interior was used to create the exact design for the film To Kill a Mockingbird, the famous book written by Lee and a telling example of the injustices black people had to endure. She grew up in Monroeville as did Truman Capote, the writer of Breakfast at Tiffanys, who happened to live next door to her.

After an overnight stay in Natchez, we are visiting an antebellum today, one of the enormous homes owned by the people who made their money from the slave trade A visit to a cotton plantation a few days ago had given us an insight into the conditions slaves lived and worked in, but today is very different. As soon we step across the threshold, the size and opulence of the home hits you in the face. I feel uncomfortable just being there, knowing how the wealth was accumulated. It doesn't feel right, being inside one.

Our stay in Montgomery is the last stop on the itinerary and gives me more opportunity to learn about the Civil Rights movement. I take a walk in the late afternoon after we arrive; it is drizzling a little but pleasantly warm. Commerce Street around the corner of the hotel runs from the river front and railroad to where the slave auctions were held. Montgomery had a larger slave population than either Natchez or New Orleans, large plaques on the sidewalk explain the street's significance; slaves arrived by boat or by railroad and then were marched, in chains, up to where I'm standing. Here they were bid for before being taken off to the plantations. I wander down to the river, crossing the railroad tracks, and imagine how frightening the experience must have been.

On a tour of Montgomery the next day, we learn about the significant role the city played in the Civil Rights movement. We see the department store front where Rosa Parks worked as a seamstress, although no longer a store, there is a statue of her diminutive figure at the exact same spot where she boarded the bus, and a museum bearing her name at the point where she was ejected. Evidently, she had to move to Detroit after the incident because of hostilities towards her.

The part of the morning tour I find most moving is when we visit the now disused Greyhound bus station. Here, in 1961, freedom riders challenging segregation laws were attacked by white suprematists. The bricked-up station now has boards with comments on about these acts. One is titled Voice of Change and reads, *'These activists endured near death beatings, jail time, and humiliation. In the end, their journeys gave a new voice to a long struggle against racism. Would you join a freedom ride today?'*

The words of Maya Angelou covering a wall over a parking lot says it all for me. *'History, despite its wrenching pain, cannot be unlived but if faced with courage, need not be lived again.'* The visit to Montgomery has been a fitting end to the trip and has given me a clearer understanding of the struggle for equality black people had to endure.

We're at Atlanta airport waiting for our flight home; I shall miss my fellow travellers, dance partners and drinking pals. What a magical holiday it's turned out to be. From the moment we arrived in Nashville, there was dancing. Music, I expected, because of the itinerary, but as soon as we hit the famous country and western city, it all yee-hawed off. And by chance, we even end the holiday dancing. One of the group mentions he is having Argentine tango lessons. Three of us immediately ask him to teach us, and he does. We're shown a basic sequence and then take it in turn to partner him. What a perfect way to spend the last hour of my holiday.

On the tour, nobody has treated me or the other three solo travellers in the group like we are pariahs. Quite the opposite! Our brilliant tour manager, Rozie, had helped us to gel by setting up the WhatsApp group. There was no obligation to be a part of it if anyone chose not to, but the platform did provide us with the chance to share information; there's a great bar playing live music, just had a tasty Chinese meal, try out this restaurant, free entry to the museum from four pm today, or even something as simple as, we'll be in the bar from five for Happy Hour if anyone wants to join us.

Much as I enjoy creating my own holiday itinerary, there's a lot to be said for escorted tours, whether travelling solo or with a companion, and they do provide a midway choice instead of going it completely alone. And what a blast the holiday turned out to be. I've already booked to go on another, this time to Japan and South Korea. Watch this space!

The holiday was undertaken in September 2024

Special to be at the Grand Ole Opry

Statue of Kunta Kinte from Alex Haley's Roots

Inside Gracelands- Presley's pool room

Acknowledgements

My gratitude to southamerica.travel for organising my South America tour, to Jasmine Travel who was responsible for planning my Central America trip, and to Titan Travel for the Southern Sights and Sounds holiday. Thank you to all the guides, drivers, and tour managers on my various trips. Your expertise and support, often going out of your way to make my holidays memorable, are much appreciated. Lastly, my thanks to Ben for suggesting the book title and for his help in creating the book cover.

About the author

JL Coley is a retired teacher living in south London. Her interests include travel, dance, sport, and the theatre. Her second book on travel, Seventy-Six Living For Kicks, about her solo adventures in Asia, is due to be published in 2026.

 @jancoley48

Printed in Dunstable, United Kingdom